ITALIAN COOKING SCHOOL

ICE CREAM

ITALIAN COOKING SCHOOL

ICE CREAM

THE SILVER SPOON KITCHEN

7 THE BIG CHILL

9 TYPES OF COLD DESSERTS

10 INGREDIENTS

12 EQUIPMENT

14 THE PROCESS

16 ICE CREAMS

66 SORBETS

86 FROZEN DESSERTS

126 CHILLED DESSERTS

174 INDEX

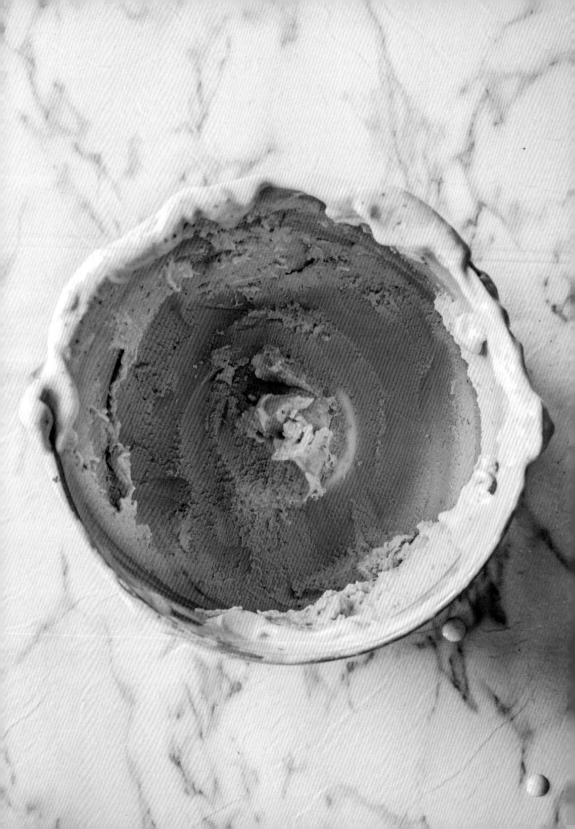

THE BIG CHILL

The preparation of ice cream, along with other frozen desserts, is steeped in a long-standing tradition. While historians documented that Roman emperors reveled in frozen desserts that resembled sorbets or Italian ices, the first true ice cream, with its use of milk and cream, is credited to the Neapolitans when it had been documented in an eighteenth century cookbook. Once ice cream had been discovered, its popularity spread across the nation and continent instantly.

Making homemade ice cream is easier than you might think. It requires the freshest ingredients available and, of course, an ice cream maker, which you will discover to be indispensable. Copious options are available in today's market, but it is important you choose a style of maker that's right for you.

Italian Cooking School Ice Cream presents an array of delicious frozen treats. From indulgent ice creams and refreshing sorbets to novel frozen and chilled desserts, each chapter opens with step-by-step directions for basic recipes and features a collection of enticing recipes to satisfy every palette. Best of all, the flavors are only limited to your imagination, and we encourage you to experiment with different combinations (fruits, spices, herbs)—the results may just surprise you.

Whether you're after a summertime favorite, such as Mint and Chocolate Ice Cream (see page 21) or a crowd-pleasing Raspberry Semifreddo (see page 108), all the recipes are designed for sharing with family and friends—as a dessert at the end of a casual meal or an eventful celebration. You will be churning cool summer treats in no time with recipes that will tantalize the most discerning taste buds.

TYPES OF COLD DESSERTS

ICE CREAM

Fresh fruit, milk, eggs, and sugar are all you need to churn up delicious homemade ice cream recipes for your next summer fête. The differences between Italian gelato and American ice cream are subtle but make the world of difference to texture and flavor. Gelato is soft, pure, and vibrant—often made with milk instead of cream, and rich with egg yolks. It has less air whipped into it than ice cream and is much denser as a result.

We recommend a freezing time of 3 hours for most of the ice cream recipes and to let it stand for 10–15 minutes to give it a creamier texture and better flavor.

SORBET

Refreshing and appetizing, sorbet is semi-thick in consistency and generally made with sugar syrup mixed with fruit juice or pulp, wine, or liqueur. It was traditionally served between courses, because it cleanses the palate. These days, it is more often served at the end of a meal.

OTHER FROZEN DESSERTS

Other frozen desserts include ice pops (lollies), which are refreshing, easy to make, and fun to eat, as well as granitas—coarse, icy desserts made with sugar, water, and flavorings such as peach (page 97) or coffee (page 101). Lighter and softer in consistency than ice cream, semifreddos can be made with cream, Italian meringue, sugar, and egg yolks. Take it out of the refrigerator 10–15 minutes before serving and always eat with a spoon.

CHILLED DESSERTS

Chilled desserts, those which are refrigerated, can be prepared ahead of time, making them ideal for entertaining and parties. Whether it's the Ricotta and Apricot Cream (page 141) or melt-in-the-mouth Tiramisu (page 162), you can taste the love in these Italian dessert recipes.

INGREDIENTS

MILK	Because milk is made up mostly of water, it will freeze into ice crystals and make ice cream icy and hard, but using milk instead of just cream also makes the finished ice cream light.
EGG YOLK	Ice creams made with egg yolks are dense, custardy, and less likely to be icy (because the egg proteins contain natural emulsifiers which bind fat and water molecules together). When preparing the custard for some recipes, such as Banana Ice Cream (page 22), be sure not to boil the mixture or the yolk will scramble and the custard will be unusable. It is important to cook custard over low heat, stirring constantly. Alternatively, cook it in a double boiler or large heatproof bowl set over a saucepan of barely simmering water—the bottom of the bowl must not touch the water).
SUGAR	Sugar not only helps to enhance the flavor, but also softens the final product. By adding sugar to ice cream, you lower the freezing point, which prevents ice cream from being cold enough to freeze in a solid ice block.
CREAM	The addition of cream will make your ice cream taste richer because high fat causes flavor to release more slowly and makes for a long-lasting flavor.
FLAVORING INGREDIENTS	Fruit is rich in vitamins, has a high water content (which makes you feel full), and minimal calories. The result can be light and refreshing, such as Fruits of the Forest Ice Cream (page 25). Other tasty ingredients range from traditional options—chocolate, coffee, or nuts— to the more daring, including Parmesan Ice Cream (page 62) or Basil Sorbet (page 85).

EQUIPMENT

ICE CREAM MAKER

Most ice cream makers, designed for home use, come with an integrated freezer bowl that needs to be prefrozen. More sophisticated models remove this step and come in handy if you're short on time, but the convenience comes at a greater cost and size. It is always advisable to follow the quantities given meticulously as well as the method indicated in the directions.

PANS AND MOLDS

Once churned, ice cream can be transferred into a pan or mold. We've used an 8 × 4-inch (20 × 10-cm) loaf pan purely for style but any size or shape will do as long as it's a freezer-safe, airtight container.

ICE POP (LOLLY) MOLDS

Ice pop (lolly) molds can be made of metal, plastic, or silicone. While they all deliver the same results, ice pops tend to release easier in silicone trays.

PLASTIC WRAP (CLINGFILM)

For semifreddos and other frozen desserts, which need to be removed from their mold before serving, we recommend lining your mold or pan with plastic wrap (clingfilm) before you transfer the ice cream to the pan. Be sure to leave a generous overhang on each side, which serves to cover the top of the dessert.

WHISKS AND FORKS

Balloon whisks are handy for incorporating ingredients or when making egg yolk custards, but you will find forks indispensable for blending, tasting, prodding, and manipulating.

Grittiness is an unpleasant texture in ice creams and sorbets, especially if it's finely ground coffee. When recipes call for pureed or blended fruit, use a strainer (sieve) to strain out the tiny pieces—the result is a smoother texture to your dessert.

THE PROCESS

Ice cream making has come a long way since it was first enjoyed by Roman emperors—particularly, with the advent of modern-day ice cream makers, which minimize freezing time so much so that ice cream can be served within 30 minutes of preparation.

When churning the mixture, you are, in fact, developing a network of ice crystals as small as possible. Once you have completed this step, the freezing process facilitates the formation of the small crystals, which results in a smooth, creamy ice cream that's not too cold on the palate. While not essential, pre-chilling the mixture improves the results of your ice cream and sorbet and results in less icy desserts. (When churning the cold mixture, the freezing occurs more quickly and finer ice crystals are formed.)

After churning, only about half of the water in your ice cream mix has turned to ice. You may need to freeze the rest of the water to have a smooth, storable block of ice cream. We have suggested 3 hours for most of the recipes but, of course, the ice cream, sorbets, and frozen desserts can be eaten sooner.

With so many types of machines available, it's important to follow the manufacturer's directions for preparation, storage, and cleaning. Some makers have a considerable bulk, so think about the size of these appliances—they may require a generous degree of storage space.

ICE CREAMS

19 EGG CUSTARD AND CHOCOLATE ICE CREAM

21 MINT AND CHOCOLATE ICE CREAM

22 BANANA ICE CREAM

25 FRUITS OF THE FOREST ICE CREAM

27 TANGERINE ICE CREAM

29 PINEAPPLE ICE CREAM

30 PEACH ICE CREAM

33 CANTALOUPE FROZEN YOGURT

34 PISTACHIO ICE CREAM WITH WILD STRAWBERRIES

37 COFFEE ICE CREAM

38 TEA ICE CREAM

41 COOKIES AND CREAM ICE CREAM

42 STRAWBERRY ICE CREAM

45 BLUEBERRY FROZEN YOGURT

46 PRALINE ICE CREAM

49 CARAMEL ICE CREAM

50 WILD STRAWBERRY AND LEMON ICE CREAM

53 NOUGAT ICE CREAM WITH GOLDEN RAISINS AND WINE

54 ROSE PETAL AND CREAM ICE CREAM

57 ZABAGLIONE ICE CREAM

58 AMARETTO ICE CREAM

61 MALAGA WINE ICE CREAM

62 PARMESAN ICE CREAM

65 JASMINE ICE CREAM

STEP 1

STEP 2

STEP 3

STEP 4

TECHNIQUE

GELATO ALLA CREMA E CIOCCOLATO
EGG CUSTARD AND CHOCOLATE ICE CREAM

EASY

– Preparation time: *5 minutes
+ 3 hours chilling, 30 minutes
churning and
3 hours freezing*
– Cooking time: *15 minutes*
– Calories per serving: *390*
– *Serves 4*

INGREDIENTS

– 1 vanilla bean (pod)
– 1¼ cups (10 fl oz/300 ml)
milk
– 6 egg yolks
– 1 pinch of salt
– ½ cup (4 oz/120 g) sugar
– 1¼ cups (10 fl oz/300 ml)
heavy (double) cream
– 3½ oz/100 g semisweet
(plain) chocolate, finely
chopped
– crisp wafers, to serve

STEP 1

Using a small knife, split the vanilla bean (pod) in half lengthwise and scrape out the seeds with the knife blade into a saucepan and add the vanilla bean. Pour in the milk and heat over low heat for about 5 minutes, or until warm.

STEP 2

Whisk the egg yolks with the salt and sugar in a large bowl until pale and frothy. Drizzle the milk over the mixture, mixing with a metal spoon, then add the cream. Cook the custard in a double boiler or heatproof bowl set over a saucepan of simmering water over low heat, stirring frequently, for about 10 minutes, or until it coats the back of a wooden spoon. Discard the vanilla bean, transfer to a bowl, and let cool. To make chocolate ice cream, add the chopped chocolate and stir until melted. Refrigerate for 3 hours.

STEP 3

Pour the mixture into an ice cream maker and churn for about 30 minutes, or according to the manufacturer's directions. Transfer the ice cream to a mold and freeze for about 3 hours, until solid.

STEP 4

Serve the ice cream with a crisp wafer.

Tip: If you prefer to cook the custard over direct heat, pour it into a heavy saucepan and cook over low heat, stirring continuously. When it starts to thicken, turn off the heat immediately (it must not boil), and let cool in a double boiler above water and ice cubes (or in a bowl set over a saucepan and ice cubes).

GELATO ALLA MENTA E CIOCCOLATO
MINT AND CHOCOLATE ICE CREAM

EASY

– Preparation time: *5 minutes
  + 20 minutes cooling,
  4 hours chilling, 25 minutes
  churning, and 3 hours freezing*
– Cooking time: *20 minutes*
– Calories per serving: *470*
– *Serves 4–6*

INGREDIENTS

– generous 2 cups (17 oz/
  500 ml) milk
– 3 cups (5 oz/150 g) small
  mint leaves
– 6 egg yolks
– ⅔ cup (4½ oz/130 g)
  superfine (caster) sugar
– 9 oz/250 g semisweet (plain)
  chocolate, broken into
  pieces
– 4–6 wafer cones, to serve
  (optional)

Bring the milk to a boil in a heavy saucepan, add the mint leaves, remove from the heat, stir, and let cool, then discard the mint leaves.

Whisk the egg yolks and sugar together in another heavy saucepan until pale and frothy, then gradually whisk in the cooled mint-flavored milk. Cook gently in a double boiler or over low heat (it must never come to a boil) for about 10 minutes, or until the custard thickens and coats the back of a wooden spoon. Remove from the heat and let cool. Refrigerate for 3 hours.

Pour the cooled mixture into an ice cream maker and churn for about 25 minutes, or according to the manufacturer's directions. Stir in the chocolate pieces. Transfer the ice cream to a container and freeze for 3 hours, until solid.

Serve in bowls or cones.

Tip: When you cook the custard, you must not let it boil, or the yolks will scramble and the custard mixture will be unusable. It is important to cook it over low heat, stirring constantly. Alternatively, cook it in a double boiler or large bowl set over a saucepan of barely simmering water.

GELATO ALLA BANANA
BANANA ICE CREAM

EASY

– Preparation time: *10 minutes
  + 4 hours chilling, 30 minutes
  churning, and 3 hours freezing*
– Cooking time: *20 minutes*
– Calories per serving: *316*
– *Serves 4*

INGREDIENTS

– ½ cup (4 fl oz/120 ml) milk
– 3 egg yolks
– scant ⅔ cup (4 oz/120 g)
  superfine (caster) sugar
– 1 cup (8 fl oz/250 ml) heavy
  (double) cream
– 6 ripe bananas, pureed

Bring the milk to a boil in a heavy saucepan, then remove from the heat.

Whisk the egg yolks with the sugar in another heavy saucepan until it is pale and frothy. Continue stirring and gradually add the hot milk in a thin stream. Cook over low heat (it must never come to a boil) for about 10 minutes, or until the custard thickens and coats the back of a spoon. Remove from the heat and let cool. Refrigerate for 4 hours.

Using an electric mixer, whip the cream until soft peaks form (when the peaks are just starting to hold, but melt back into themselves after a second). Fold the cream and pureed banana into the cooled custard mixture.

Pour the mixture into an ice cream maker and churn for about 30 minutes, or according to the manufacturer's directions. Transfer the ice cream to a mold and freeze for about 3 hours, until solid.

GELATO AI FRUTTI DI BOSCO
FRUITS OF THE FOREST ICE CREAM

EASY

– Preparation time: *10 minutes
+ 4 hours chilling, 30 minutes
churning, and 3 hours freezing*
– Calories per serving: *280*
– *Serves 4–6*

INGREDIENTS

– 2¾ cups (14 oz/400 g)
mixed berries, such as
strawberries, blackberries,
raspberries, and blueberries
– juice of ½ lemon, strained
– 1 cup (7 oz/200 g) superfine
(caster) sugar
– 1 cup (8 fl oz/250 ml) heavy
(double) cream

Put the berries, lemon juice, sugar, and cream into a
blender and puree for 2 minutes. Refrigerate for 4 hours.

Pour the mixture into an ice cream maker and churn for
about 30 minutes, or according to the manufacturer's
directions. Transfer the ice cream in a mold and freeze for
about 3 hours, until solid.

Scoop the ice cream into bowls to serve.

GELATO AL MANDARINO
TANGERINE ICE CREAM

- Preparation time: *35 minutes*
  + 30 minutes churning and
  4 hours freezing
- Calories per serving: *122*
- *Serves 4*

INGREDIENTS

- juice of 15 tangerines, the
  peels reserved (see Note)
- ⅔ cup (5 fl oz/150 ml) milk
- scant ⅔ cup (4 oz/120 g)
  superfine (caster) sugar
- chopped pistachios, to
  decorate

Pour the tangerine juice, milk, and sugar into a blender and blend thoroughly. Refrigerate for 4 hours.

Pour the mixture into an ice cream maker and churn for about 30 minutes, or according to the manufacturer's directions. Transfer the ice cream to a mold and freeze for about 3 hours, until solid.

Serve the ice cream in the tangerine cups or in glasses, decorated with chopped pistachios.

Note: To make cups from the peel, cut off the upper part of the tangerines to form a lid, scoop out the flesh without damaging the peel, squeeze the flesh, and proceed as above. Once you have made the ice cream, fill the cups, freeze the tangerines for 30 minutes, and serve.

GELATO ALL'ANANAS
PINEAPPLE ICE CREAM

EASY

– Preparation time: *15 minutes
+ 4 hours chilling, 30 minutes
churning, and 3 hours freezing*
– Calories per serving: *208*
– *Serves 4*

INGREDIENTS

– 1 large fresh pineapple
– 1 (8 oz/227 g) can pineapple
chunks in syrup
– 1 tablespoon confectioners'
(icing) sugar
– 1 cup (8 fl oz/250 ml) heavy
(double) cream, softly
whipped

Slice the top off the pineapple, then remove the skin, core, and tougher parts. Put the pineapple flesh and chunks in syrup into a blender or food processor and blend together. Add the confectioners' (icing) sugar and stir. Refrigerate for 4 hours.

Pour the mixture into an ice cream maker and churn for about 30 minutes, or according to the manufacturer's directions. Fold in the whipped cream.

Transfer the ice cream to a mold and freeze for about 3 hours, until solid.

Tip: You can use the fresh pineapple shell to serve the ice cream. After slicing off the top of the pineapple, halve it lengthwise. Carefully scoop out the flesh without breaking the skin, remove the core and tougher parts and proceed as above. Transfer the ice cream to the pineapple shell instead of the mold.

GELATO ALLA PESCA
PEACH ICE CREAM

EASY

– Preparation time: *10 minutes*
 + 30 minutes churning,
 6 hours chilling, and 3 hours
 freezing
– Cooking time: *5 minutes*
– Calories per serving: *354*
– *Serves 4*

INGREDIENTS

– 3 peaches, peeled, pitted,
 and sliced
– 1½ cups (6⅓ oz/180 g)
 confectioner's (icing) sugar
– 2 tablespoons dark Navy
 rum
– 2 sheets gelatin
– 5 eggs, separated

Put the peaches into a bowl, cover with the sugar, and macerate in the refrigerator for 2 hours, then push the peaches through a strainer (sieve). Meanwhile, generously brush the inside of an 8 × 4-inch (20 × 10-cm) loaf pan (tin) with rum and set aside.

In a bowl, soak the gelatin in 1 cup (8 fl oz/250 ml) cold water.

Put the egg yolks into a heavy saucepan over low heat. Add the peach puree, and cook over medium heat for about 5 minutes, stirring constantly, until thickened.

Put the gelatin and soaking water in a double boiler or a heatproof bowl set over a saucepan of gently simmering water, making sure the bottom of the bowl doesn't touch the water, until it has dissolved. Add it to the peach mixture and let cool. Refrigerate for 4 hours.

Beat the egg whites in a grease-free bowl or electric mixer to stiff peaks and fold the stiffly beaten egg whites into the cooled peach mixture. Pour the mixture into an ice cream maker and churn for about 30 minutes, or according to the manufacturer's directions. Transfer the ice cream to the prepared pan and freeze for about 3 hours, or until solid. Slice and serve.

CREMA GELATA AL MELONE
MELON ICE CREAM

EASY

– Preparation time: *15 minutes + 30 minutes churning and 3 hours freezing*
– Calories per serving: *134*
– *Serves 2*

INGREDIENTS

– 2 small ripe cantaloupe melons
– 3 tablespoons wildflower honey, or to taste
– scant ½ cup (3½ oz/100 g) plain (natural) yogurt
– confectioner's (icing) sugar
– mint leaf, to garnish

Cut 1 melon in half, remove seeds, and scoop the flesh out with a spoon. Put the melon flesh into a blender or food processor and process to a puree, then pour it into a bowl. Add the honey, taste, and adjust to your desired sweetness. Add the yogurt and stir gently until it is thoroughly combined. Refrigerate for 4 hours.

Pour the mixture into an ice cream maker and churn for about 30 minutes, or according to the manufacturer's directions. Transfer the ice cream to a mold and freeze for about 3 hours, until solid.

Meanwhile, use a melon baller to scoop out balls from the remaining melon and set aside. About 10 minutes before serving, take the ice cream out of the freezer and unmold onto a serving dish. Serve in slices, dust with confectioners' (icing) sugar, and decorate with the melon balls. Finish with a mint leaf.

GELATO AL PISTACCHIO CON FRAGOLINE DI BOSCO

PISTACHIO ICE CREAM WITH WILD STRAWBERRIES

EASY

– Preparation time: *10 minutes
  + 4 hours chilling, 30 minutes
  churning, and 3 hours freezing*
– Cooking time: *20 minutes*
– Calories per serving: *543*
– *Serves 4*

INGREDIENTS

– 3 cups (25 fl oz/750 ml) milk
– 1 cup (7 oz/200 g) superfine
  (caster) sugar
– 1 tablespoon pistachio paste
– 8 egg yolks
– ⅓ cup (2 oz/50 g) shelled
  pistachios, chopped

FOR THE SAUCE

– juice and the grated zest of
  1 lemon
– ½ cup (3½ oz/100 g)
  superfine (caster) sugar
– 3½ cups (1 lb 2 oz/500 g)
  wild or regular strawberries,
  hulled and halved

TO DECORATE

– wild or regular strawberries
– 2 tablespoons (¾ oz/20 g)
  pistachio nuts

Bring the milk to a boil in a heavy saucepan. Add half the sugar and the pistachio paste, stir, then remove from the heat and let infuse for 10 minutes.

Whisk the egg yolks and remaining sugar in another heavy saucepan, then while stirring, gradually drizzle the milk into the egg mixture. Cook gently in a double boiler or over low heat (it must never come to a boil) for about 10 minutes, or until the custard thickens and coats the back of a wooden spoon. Remove from the heat, strain the custard into a bowl, and let cool. Refrigerate for 4 hours.

Add the chopped pistachio nuts to the custard, then pour the mixture into an ice cream maker and churn for about 30 minutes, or according to the manufacturer's directions. Transfer the ice cream to a mold and freeze for about 3 hours, until solid.

Meanwhile, make the sauce. Put 2 tablespoons lemon juice and a little grated lemon zest in a skillet or frying pan. Add the sugar and cook over low heat for 5 minutes, or until a syrup has formed. Add the halved strawberries to the syrup, then remove from the heat.

Pour the strawberry sauce into individual glasses or dishes and add 2 scoops of ice cream. Decorate with more strawberries and pistachios and serve immediately.

Tip: To remove the purple skin from the pistachios, blanch the nuts for a few minutes in boiling water, drain, and rub them in a kitchen cloth or in paper towels.

GELATO AL CAFFÈ
COFFEE ICE CREAM

AVERAGE

– Preparation time: *35 minutes*
  + 4 hours chilling, 30 minutes
  churning, and 3 hours freezing
– *Cooking time: 15 minutes*
– *Calories per serving: 550*
– *Serves 4*

INGREDIENTS

– 6 tablespoons instant coffee
– 1 cup (8 fl oz/250 ml) heavy
  (double) cream
– generous 1½ cups (13 fl oz/
  375 ml) milk
– 5 egg yolks
– ¾ cup (5 oz/150 g) superfine
  (caster) sugar

Dilute the instant coffee in 3 tablespoons water. Heat the cream, milk, and coffee in a heavy saucepan over medium-low heat and stir gently with a wooden spoon. When little bubbles start to form, remove from the heat. Strain into a clean saucepan and keep warm.

In a large bowl, whisk the egg yolks and sugar until pale and frothy, then gradually stir in the milk-and-coffee mixture. Mix well.

Cook the custard in a double boiler or in a heatproof bowl set over a saucepan of barely simmering water over low heat, stirring frequently, for about 10 minutes, or until it coats the back of a wooden spoon. Refrigerate for 4 hours.

Pour the mixture into an ice cream maker and churn for about 30 minutes, or according to the manufacturer's directions. Transfer the ice cream to a mold and freeze for about 3 hours, until solid.

Remove the ice cream from the freezer about 10 minutes before serving.

Tip: If you prefer to cook the custard over direct heat, pour it into a heavy saucepan and cook over low heat, stirring continuously. When it starts to thicken, turn off the heat immediately (it must not boil), and let cool in a double boiler above water and ice cubes (or in a bowl set over a saucepan and ice cubes).

GELATO AL TÈ
TEA ICE CREAM

EASY

– *Preparation time: 20 minutes
+ 30 minutes churning,
15 minutes cooling, and
4 hours freezing*
– Cooking time: *25 minutes*
– Calories per serving: *169*
– *Serves* 4

INGREDIENTS

– 6 eggs yolks
– 1½ cups (11 oz/300 g) granulated (caster) sugar
– 1 cup (8 fl oz/250 ml) strong black tea, boiling
– generous 2 cups (17 fl oz/ 500 ml) milk
– rolled wafers, to serve (optional)

Whisk the egg yolks gently with the sugar in a bowl until pale and frothy. Gradually add the boiling tea and milk, whisking continuously. Cook gently in a double boiler or over low heat (it must never come to a boil) for about 10 minutes, or until the custard thickens and coats the back of a wooden spoon. Refrigerate for 4 hours.

Pour the mixture into an ice cream maker and churn for about 30 minutes, or according to the manufacturer's directions. Transfer the ice cream to a mold and freeze for about 3 hours, until solid. Serve with round wafers, if using.

GELATO AI BISCOTTI E YOGURT

COOKIES AND CREAM ICE CREAM

EASY

- Preparation time: *10 minutes
  + 30 minutes churning,
  4 hours 30 minutes chilling,
  and 3 hours freezing*
- Calories per serving: *403*
- *Serves 6*

INGREDIENTS

- 1⅓ cups (5 oz/150 g) coarse
  dry cookie (biscuit) crumbs
- 2 tablespoons dark Navy
  rum
- scant ½ cup (3½ oz/100 g)
  plain (natural) yogurt
- scant ¼ cup (2 fl oz/50 ml)
  heavy (double) cream
- ¾ cup (5 oz/150 g) superfine
  (caster) sugar
- 1 teaspoon vanilla sugar
  (see Note)
- 2 oz/50 g semisweet (plain)
  chocolate, slivered (flaked)
- ⅔ cup (2¾ oz/75 g) chopped
  hazelnuts

Put the cookie (biscuit) crumbs into a bowl, sprinkle with the rum, and chill in the refrigerator for 30 minutes.

Meanwhile, in another bowl, beat the yogurt with the cream, sugar, and vanilla sugar until increased in volume and frothy. Add the cookie crumbs, slivered (flaked) semisweet (plain) chocolate and chopped hazelnuts and stir in to combine. Refrigerate for 4 hours.

Pour the mixture into an ice cream maker and churn for about 30 minutes, or according to the manufacturer's directions. Transfer the ice cream to a mold and freeze for about 3 hours, until solid.

Tip: For a nonalcoholic option, instead of soaking the cookies (biscuits) in the rum, chop them and soak them in a small glass of unsweetened almond milk or apple juice.

Note: To make vanilla sugar, combine confectioners' (icing) sugar with the seeds from a vanilla bean (pod), or store the sugar in a jar with a slit vanilla bean for about a week.

GELATO ALLA FRAGOLA
STRAWBERRY ICE CREAM

AVERAGE

– Preparation time: *30 minutes
+ 4 hours chilling, 30 minutes
churning, 10 minutes cooling,
and 3 hours freezing*
– Cooking time: *35 minutes*
– Calories per serving: *505–379*
– *Serves 6–8*

INGREDIENTS

– 4¼ cups (1 lb 5 oz/600 g)
strawberries, hulled
– 1 tablespoon orange blossom
water
– 1 tablespoon lemon juice
– scant ⅔ cup (3½ oz/120 g)
superfine (caster) sugar
– 4 egg yolks
– 1¼ cups (10 fl oz/300 ml)
heavy (double) cream

FOR THE STRAWBERRY SAUCE (OPTIONAL)

– scant 4¼ cups (1 lb 5 oz/
600 g) strawberries, hulled
– ½ cup (4 oz/120 g) plain
(natural) yogurt
– generous ⅓ cup (3 oz/80 g)
superfine sugar

FOR THE RASPBERRY SAUCE (OPTIONAL)

– 2½ cups (11 oz/300 g)
raspberries
– 2 tablespoons superfine sugar
– 1 tablespoon orange blossom
water

Puree the strawberries into a blender, add the orange blossom water, lemon juice, and ¼ cup (1½ oz/40 g) of the sugar.

In a bowl, beat the egg yolks with the remaining sugar until pale and frothy, then add the cream. Cook gently in a double boiler or over low heat (do not let it boil) for 10 minutes, or until it coats the back of a wooden spoon. Refrigerate for 4 hours.

Pour the custard into the blender with the pureed strawberries and blend until mixed together. Pour the mixture into an ice cream maker and churn for about 30 minutes, or according to the manufacturer's directions. Rinse a mold with cold water, then transfer the ice cream to the mold and freeze for about 3 hours, until solid.

Meanwhile, make the strawberry sauce. Puree the strawberries in a blender, then put into a bowl, add the yogurt, sugar, and scant ½ cup (3½ fl oz/100 ml) water, and mix together. Chill in the refrigerator.

To make the raspberry cream, push the raspberries through a strainer (sieve) into a bowl, add the sugar and orange blossom water, and stir until combined.

Remove the ice cream from the freezer and serve it in glasses or small dishes with the raspberry cream and strawberry sauce poured over the top.

GELATO ALLO YOGURT CON MIRTILLI

BLUEBERRY FROZEN YOGURT

EASY

- Preparation time: *15 minutes
  + 4 hours chilling, 30 minutes
  churning, and 3 hours freezing*
- Cooking time: *5 minutes*
- Calories per serving: *169*
- *Serves 6*

INGREDIENTS

- 2 tablespoons dry
  unsweetened (desiccated)
  coconut
- 3⅓ cups (1 lb 2 oz/500 g)
  blueberries, plus extra to
  garnish
- 1 teaspoon lime or lemon
  juice
- 1 teaspoon vanilla sugar (see
  page 41)
- scant 1 cup (7¾ fl oz/
  225 ml) plain (natural)
  yogurt
- 2 tablespoons honey
- scant ½ cup (3½ fl oz/
  100 ml) heavy (double)
  cream, chilled
- coconut chips, to serve
  (optional)

Lightly toast the coconut in a dry nonstick skillet or
frying pan over low-medium heat for 2 minutes, or until
lightly brown, then let cool.

Put 2 cups (11 oz/300 g) blueberries into a blender or food
processor with the lime or lemon juice and the vanilla
sugar and puree slowly. Add the yogurt, coconut, and
honey. Mix well.

Using an electric mixer, whip the chilled cream and fold
it into the yogurt-and-blueberry mixture. Refrigerate for
4 hours.

Pour the mixture into an ice cream maker and churn for
about 30 minutes, or according to the manufacturer's
directions. Rinse a mold with cold water, then transfer the
ice cream to the mold and freeze for about 3 hours, until
solid. Serve with blueberries and coconut chips, if using.

GELATO AL CROCCANTE DI NOCCIOLE
PRALINE ICE CREAM

AVERAGE

– Preparation time: *15 minutes*
  + 4 hours chilling, 30 minutes
  churning, and 3 hours freezing
– Cooking time: *20 minutes*
– Calories per serving: *584*
– *Serves 6*

INGREDIENTS

– 3 tablespoons milk
– 1 vanilla bean (pod), slit
  lengthwise
– 1 egg
– 2 egg yolks
– scant 1 cup (6 oz/180 g)
  superfine (caster) sugar
– ⅔ cup (5 fl oz/150 ml) light
  (single) cream
– hot chocolate sauce, to serve
  (optional)
– 6 waffle cones, to serve
  (optional)

FOR THE PRALINE

– sweet almond oil, for
  brushing
– 1 cup (7 oz/200 g) superfine
  sugar
– 1 cup (5 oz/150 g) hazelnuts,
  skinned

For the praline, brush a sheet of parchment (baking) paper with almond oil.

In a heavy saucepan over medium heat, add the milk and vanilla bean (pod) and bring to a simmer.

In a bowl, combine the whole egg, egg yolks, and sugar and whisk until pale and frothy, then gradually pour the egg mixture into the simmering milk, reduce the heat to low, and cook for 5 minutes. Remove from the heat and let cool. Refrigerate for 4 hours.

Meanwhile, make the praline. Melt the sugar in a small skillet or frying pan over low heat and when it begins to color, add the hazelnuts. Stir for 2–3 minutes, then remove from the heat and pour the mixture on the sheet of oiled parchment paper and let cool.

Pour the cooled custard and the cream into an ice cream maker and churn for about 30 minutes, or according to the manufacturer's directions.

Cover the praline with a dish towel that has been folded several times and crush it into small pieces with a meat mallet or rolling pin. Put the praline pieces into the ice cream, stir carefully, and freeze for 3 hours.

Remove the ice cream from the freezer 15 minutes before serving and serve in glasses or waffle cones with a hot chocolate sauce, if using.

GELATO AL CARAMELLO
CARAMEL ICE CREAM

AVERAGE

– Preparation time: *10 minutes*
  + 4 hours 30 minutes chilling,
  30 minutes churning, and
  3 hours freezing
– Cooking time: *30 minutes*
– Calories per serving: *389*
– *Serves 4*

INGREDIENTS

– ½ cup (3½ oz/100 g)
  superfine (caster) sugar
– 3 egg yolks
– scant 2 cups (15 fl oz/
  450 ml) double (heavy)
  cream

In a skillet or frying pan, heat the sugar and 1 tablespoon cold water over medium heat until it dissolves. Increase the heat slightly, skim off the foam, and when the syrup has turned russet, carefully pour ½ cup (4 fl oz/120 ml) hot water into the pan. Reduce to very low heat, cover, and heat for 20 minutes, or until the sugar has completely dissolved and is the consistency of a thick syrup.

Lightly beat the egg yolks in a bowl, then drizzle in the syrup, stirring vigorously, until you have a light and frothy mixture. Continue to stir until the mixture becomes cold. Refrigerate for 4 hours.

Whip the cream in a bowl or electric mixer, then fold it into the caramel-egg yolk mixture. Pour the mixture into an ice cream maker and churn for about 30 minutes, or according to the manufacturer's directions. Transfer the ice cream to a mold and freeze for about 3 hours, until solid. Serve in glasses or small dishes.

Tip: When you pour water into the caramel, remove the skillet from the heat, and be careful—it will start to boil quickly, spitting and bubbling. When the mixture has settled down, put the pan back on low heat.

GELATO ALLE FRAGOLINE E LIMONE
WILD STRAWBERRY AND LEMON ICE CREAM

AVERAGE

– Preparation time: *20 minutes + 4 hours chilling, 30 minutes churning and 3 hours freezing*
– Cooking time: *5 minutes*
– Calories per serving: *462–385*
– *Serves 10–12*

FOR THE WILD STRAWBERRY ICE CREAM

– 2¾ cups (14 oz/400 g) wild strawberries, hulled
– 1 tablespoon light white wine
– 1¼ cups (10 fl oz/300 ml) milk
– 1 lemon zest
– 1 vanilla bean (pod)
– 2 eggs
– 1¼ cups (9 oz/250 g) superfine (caster) sugar
– scant 1 cup (7 fl oz/200 ml) heavy (double) cream
– 10–12 waffle cones, to serve (optional)

FOR THE LEMON ICE CREAM

– juice of 6 unwaxed lemons
– 1¼ cups (9 oz/250 g) superfine (caster) sugar
– 1½ cups (12 fl oz/350 ml) milk
– 1½ cups (12 fl oz/350 ml) heavy (double) cream

To make the strawberry ice cream, rinse the wild strawberries briefly in the white wine. Heat the milk in a heavy saucepan with a strip of lemon zest and the whole vanilla bean (pod) over low heat and when it reaches a boil, remove from the heat and let cool. Strain into a bowl.

Whisk the eggs with the sugar in a food processor until pale and frothy. Add the wild strawberries and continue to process, then add the cream and the milk. Refrigerate for 4 hours.

To make the lemon ice cream, blend the lemon juice with the sugar in a blender. Add the milk and cream and blend for a few more seconds. Refrigerate for 4 hours.

Pour the strawberry mixture into an ice cream maker and churn for about 15 minutes. Pour the mixture on top of the churned layer of strawberry ice cream in the ice cream maker and churn for 15 minutes.

Rinse a mold with cold water, then transfer the ice cream to the mold and freeze for about 3 hours, until solid. Serve in bowls or waffle cones, if using.

GELATO AL TORRONE CON UVETTE E VINO

NOUGAT ICE CREAM WITH GOLDEN RAISINS AND WINE

EASY

– Preparation time: *20 minutes
+ 1 hour soaking, 4 hours
chilling, 30 minutes churning,
and 3 hours freezing*
– Calories per serving: *581*
– *Serves 6*

INGREDIENTS

– generous ¾ cup (4 oz/
  120 g) golden raisins
  (sultanas)
– 1 cup (8 fl oz/250 ml)
  medium or sweet sherry
– generous 2 cups (17 fl oz/
  500 ml) milk
– ½ teaspoon vanilla extract
– 6 egg yolks
– 1 cup (8 fl oz/250 ml) heavy
  (double) cream
– 5 oz/150 g nougat, chopped

In a bowl, soak the golden raisins (sultanas) in the sherry for 1 hour.

To make the ice cream, combine the milk, vanilla, and egg yolks together in a bowl and mix well, then chill in the refrigerator for 4 hours.

Using an electric mixer, whip the cream to stiff peaks. Fold in the cream and nougat into the chilled milk-and-egg yolk mixture. Pour the mixture into an ice cream maker and churn for about 30 minutes or according to the manufacturer's directions. Rinse a mold with cold water, then transfer the ice cream into the mold and freeze for about 3 hours, until solid.

Serve with the sherry-soaked golden raisins.

Tip: Freeze the nougat for about an hour to make chopping easier.

GELATO ALLA PANNA E PETALI DI ROSA
ROSE PETAL AND CREAM ICE CREAM

– Preparation time: *10 minutes*
  + 3 hours standing, 30 minutes
  churning, and 3 hours freezing
– Cooking time: *10 minutes*
– Calories per serving: *300*
– *Serves 4*

INGREDIENTS

– scant 1 cup (7 fl oz/200 ml)
  champagne
– scant 1 cup (6⅓ oz/180 g)
  superfine (caster) sugar
– 3 cups (2–2½ oz/50–60 g)
  fresh unsprayed rose petals,
  plus extra for decorating
– 2–3 drops rose extract
– scant ½ cup (3½ fl oz/
  100 ml) heavy (double)
  cream

Pour the champagne and scant ½ cup (3½ fl oz/100 ml) water into a saucepan and heat gently over low heat. Add the sugar, stirring constantly, for 5 minutes or until it has dissolved. Remove from the heat and stir in half the rose petals into the syrup. Let stand for 3 hours to let the flavors mingle.

Strain the syrup into a bowl and add the remaining petals and the rose extract. Pour the mixture into a blender and blend well, then pour into an ice cream maker.

Using an electric mixer, whip the cream to stiff peaks. Stir the whipped cream into the syrup mixture and churn for about 30 minutes, or according to the manufacturer's directions. Rinse a mold with cold water, then transfer the ice cream to the mold and freeze for about 3 hours, until solid.

Scoop the ice cream into dessert bowls or glasses, decorate with rose petals, and serve immediately.

GELATO ALLO ZABAIONE
ZABAGLIONE ICE CREAM

AVERAGE

– Preparation time: *30 minutes*
  + 30 minutes churning and
  4 hours freezing
– Cooking time: *15 minutes*
– Calories per serving: *599*
– *Serves 8*

INGREDIENTS

– 6 egg yolks
– ⅔ cup (4½ oz/130 g)
  superfine (caster) sugar
– scant ½ cup (3½ fl oz/
  100 ml) Marsala or port
– 3 cups (25 fl oz/750 ml)
  whipped cream

In a heavy saucepan, whisk the eggs and sugar until pale and frothy. Add the port and cook over low heat, stirring constantly for 10 minutes until the zabaglione thickens. Make sure the mixture doesn't boil. Remove from the heat and let cool.

Gently fold in the whipped cream into the zabaglione, stirring slowly from the bottom to the top. Refrigerate for 4 hours.

Pour the mixture into an ice cream maker and churn for about 30 minutes, or according to the manufacturer's directions. Transfer to the mold, then freeze for about 3 hours, until solid.

Tip: If you are not used to making zabaglione, make it in a large double boiler large or heatproof bowl over a saucepan of simmering water or so the mixture doesn't overheat and scramble the egg yolks.

GELATO ALL'AMARETTO
AMARETTO ICE CREAM

AVERAGE

– Preparation time: *40 minutes*
  + 30 minutes churning and
  4 hours freezing
– Cooking time: *10 minutes*
– Calories per serving: *577*
– *Serves 4*

INGREDIENTS

– ½ cup (2¾ oz/75 g) Muscat
  or dark raisins, seeded, if
  necessary, washed, and dried
– 2 tablespoons brandy
– 1 cup (8 fl oz/250 ml) milk
– 1 egg, separated
– generous ¾ cup (3½ oz/
  100 g) confectioners' (icing)
  sugar
– 12 Amaretti cookies
  (biscuits), chopped
– 1 cup (8 fl oz/250 ml) heavy
  (double) cream
– 1 pinch of salt
– 10 cherries in syrup, drained
  and coarsely chopped

TO DECORATE

– 8 small amaretti cookies
– amaretto liqueur, for soaking

Put the raisins into a bowl, add the brandy, and let macerate for 10 minutes.

Put the milk and egg yolk into a double boiler or a heavy saucepan and beat for 5 minutes, then cook over very low heat, beating constantly, until the mixture thickens (don't let the mixture boil). Gradually add the confectioners' (icing) sugar, then remove from the heat and continue stirring until the mixture has completely cooled.

Whip the cream in a bowl or electric mixer to stiff peaks, then in another bowl, whisk the egg white and salt together until stiff.

Add the amaretti cookies (biscuits) to the custard mixture and mix, then add the chopped cherries, egg white, and the drained and squeezed raisins. Stir until everything is mixed in. Refrigerate for 4 hours.

Transfer the mixture to an ice cream maker and churn for 30 minutes, or according to the manufacturer's directions. Transfer to the mold, then freeze for about 3 hours, until solid.

About 30 minutes before serving, soak the amaretti cookies in a little liqueur. Serve the ice cream with the amaretti cookies.

GELATO AL VINO DI MALAGA
MALAGA WINE ICE CREAM

EASY

- Preparation time: *30 minutes + 4 hours chilling, 30 minutes churning, and 3 hours freezing*
- Cooking time: *30 minutes*
- Calories per serving: *416*
- *Serves 4*

INGREDIENTS

- 1 cup (8 fl oz/250 ml) milk
- ⅓ cup (2¾ oz/70 g) superfine (caster) sugar
- ½ teaspoon vanilla extract
- 2 egg yolks
- ⅔ cup (5 fl oz/150 ml) Malaga wine
- ½ cup (4 fl oz/120 ml) heavy (double) cream

TO DECORATE

- 1 orange, very thinly sliced
- Maraschino cherries
- wafers

In a heavy saucepan, combine the milk, sugar, and vanilla and bring to a boil. Remove the pan from the heat.

In a double boiler, without any heat, whisk the egg yolks and then add the wine in a thin stream. Continue whisking and gradually at the hot milk. Place the double boiler over low heat and cook, stirring constantly, until the mixture thickens. This will take at least 20 minutes. Alternatively, use a heatproof bowl set over a saucepan of simmering water. Remove from the heat and let the custard cool, still stirring constantly.

Using an electric mixer, whip the cream to stiff peaks, and then add it to the custard. Refrigerate for 4 hours.

Pour the mixture into an ice cream maker and churn for about 30 minutes, or according to the manufacturer's directions. Transfer the ice cream to the mold and freeze for about 3 hours, until solid.

When ready to serve, unmold the ice cream onto a serving dish and decorate it with orange slices, cherries, and wafers.

GELATO AL PARMIGIANO

PARMESAN ICE CREAM

EASY

– Preparation time: *10 minutes
+ 5 hours chilling, 30 minutes
churning, and 3 hours freezing*
– Cooking time: *10 minutes*
– Calories per serving: *653*
– *Serves 4*

INGREDIENTS

– generous 2 cups (17 fl oz/
500 ml) heavy (double)
cream
– scant ⅔ cup (4 oz/120 g)
raw cane sugar
– 1½ cups (4 oz/120 g) grated
Parmesan cheese

In a heavy pan, combine the cream and sugar and bring to a boil over low heat, stirring frequently. Remove from the heat and add the Parmesan cheese, stirring constantly until the cheese has completely melted. Pour the mixture into a large bowl, cover with plastic wrap (clingfilm), and refrigerate for 4 hours.

Pour the mixture into an ice cream maker and churn for about 30 minutes, or according to the manufacturer's directions. Rinse a mold with cold water, then transfer the ice cream to the mold and freeze for about 3 hours, until solid. Serve in a glass bowl.

Tip: You can also flavor the cream with rosemary or lemon thyme leaves.

GELATO AI FIORI DI GELSOMINO
JASMINE ICE CREAM

EASY

– Preparation time: *30 minutes
+ 4 hours chilling, 10 minutes
cooling, 30 minutes churning,
and 3 hours freezing*
– Cooking time: *10 minutes*
– Calories per serving: *280*
– *Serves 4*

INGREDIENTS

– 1 cup (7 oz/200 g) superfine
(caster) sugar
– 50–60 fresh unsprayed
jasmine flowers
– scant ½ cup (3½ fl oz/
100 ml) heavy (double)
cream
– fresh flowers, to decorate

In a heavy pan, add the sugar, jasmine flowers, and
generous 2 cups (17 fl oz/500 ml) water and bring to a
boil over medium heat, stirring for 5 minutes, or until the
sugar has dissolved. Reduce the heat to low and simmer,
without stirring, for 10 minutes. Remove from the heat
and let cool. Refrigerate for 4 hours.

Meanwhile, using an electric mixer, whip the cream to
stiff peaks. Pour the jasmine mixture and whipped cream
into an ice cream maker and churn for about 30 minutes,
or according to the manufacturer's directions. Transfer
the ice cream to a mold and freeze for about 3 hours,
until solid.

To serve, divide the ice cream among large champagne
glasses or medium highball glasses, and decorate with a
few fresh flowers.

SORBETS

69   LEMON SORBET

70   PEACH SORBET

73   ORANGE SORBET

74   PLUM SORBET

77   CHERRY SORBET

78   KIWI SORBET

81   TROPICAL SORBET

82   PROSECCO SORBET

85   BASIL SORBET

TECHNIQUE

SORBETTO AL LIMONE
LEMON SORBET

EASY

– Preparation time: *5 minutes
+ 3 hours chilling, 30 minutes
churning and
2–3 hours freezing*
– Cooking time: *10 minutes*
– Calories per serving: *200–134*
– *Serves 4–6*

INGREDIENTS

– 1¼ cups (9 oz/250 g) sugar
– 1 unwaxed lemon
– 1 cup (8 fl oz/250 ml) lemon
  juice

STEP 1

In a heavy saucepan, combine the sugar, 1 cup
(8 fl oz/250 ml) water, and a strip of lemon zest.

STEP 2

Bring to a boil over medium heat, stirring constantly
until the sugar has dissolved, then remove from the
heat and let cool. Remove the strip of lemon zest. Pour
the lemon juice through a strainer (sieve) into the pan.
Refrigerate for 3 hours.

STEP 3

Finely grate the remaining lemon zest. Transfer the
flavored sugar mixture to an ice cream maker, add the
grated lemon zest, and churn for about 30 minutes,
or according to the manufacturer's directions.

STEP 4

Eat immediately or pour into ice pop (lolly) molds and
freeze for 2–3 hours, until solid.

SORBETTO ALLA PESCA
PEACH SORBET

EASY

– Preparation time: *15 minutes + 3 hours chilling, 30 minutes churning, and 2–3 hours freezing*
– Cooking time: *15 minutes*
– Calories per serving: *689–459*
– *Serves 4–6*

INGREDIENTS

– 1 cup (8 fl oz/250 ml) champagne
– grated zest of 1 lemon
– 3 cups (1 lb 5 oz/600 g) superfine (caster) sugar
– 5–6 peaches (about 1¾ lb/ 800 g), peeled and pitted
– small mint leaves, to decorate (optional)

In a heavy saucepan, combine the champagne, 3 cups (25 fl oz/750 ml) water, lemon zest, and sugar over low heat and heat for 3–4 minutes, stirring occasionally until the sugar has dissolved. Remove from the heat and let cool.

Meanwhile, put the peaches into a blender or food processor and process to a puree. Add the puree to the syrup and stir well to mix.

Refrigerate for 3 hours. Pour the mixture into an ice cream maker and churn for about 30 minutes, or according to the manufacturer's directions. Rinse an 8 × 4-inch (20 × 10-cm) loaf pan (tin) with cold water, then transfer the sorbet to the pan and freeze for 2–3 hours, until solid.

Serve in glasses or small dishes, decorated with mint leaves, if using.

Tip: To peel peaches easily, blanch them for a few seconds in boiling water, drain, let cool, then peel off the skins.

SORBETTO ALL'ARANCIA
ORANGE SORBET

EASY

– Preparation time: *10 minutes*
  + 10 minutes cooling,
  30 minutes churning, and
  2–3 hours freezing
– *Cooking time: 20 minutes*
– Calories per serving: *294*
– *Serves 6*

INGREDIENTS

– 1 cup (7 oz/200 g) superfine
  (caster) sugar
– juice of 3 blood oranges
– juice of ½ lemon
– 2 tablespoons orange-
  flavored liqueur
– orange slices, to decorate
  (optional)

In a heavy saucepan, dissolve the sugar in 1 cup
(8 fl oz/250 ml) water over low heat. Bring to a boil,
without stirring, for 15 minutes, then remove from
the heat and let cool.

Stir the citrus juices and liqueur into the cooled syrup.
Refrigerate for 3 hours.

Pour the mixture into an ice cream maker and churn for
about 30 minutes, or according to the manufacturer's
directions. Transfer the sorbet to the mold and freeze for
about 2–3 hours, until solid.

Serve in glasses decorated with an orange slice, if using.

*Tip: To avoid the syrup becoming too thick through the
excessive evaporation of the water, boil it over low heat.
Alternatively, boil 1 cup (7 oz/200 g) sugar in 1 cup
(8 fl oz/250 ml) water for 1 minute, until the sugar
has dissolved.*

SORBETTO ALLA PRUGNA
PLUM SORBET

EASY

– Preparation time: *15 minutes
+ 3 hours chilling, 30 minutes
churning, and 2–3 hours
freezing*
– Cooking time: *10 minutes*
– Calories per serving: *300*
– *Serves 4*

INGREDIENTS

– 6 plums, halved, pitted, and
chopped
– grated zest of 1 orange
– 1¼ cups (9 oz/250 g)
superfine (caster) sugar
– ½ cinnamon stick
– 1 egg white

In a large bowl, combine the plums, grated orange zest,
and 2 tablespoons of the sugar and let stand for about
10 minutes.

Meanwhile, pour 1 cup (8 fl oz/350 ml) water into a heavy
saucepan, add the remaining sugar and the cinnamon
stick, and bring to a boil over low heat, stirring until the
sugar has dissolved. Boil, without stirring, for another
5 minutes, then remove from the heat, discard the
cinnamon stick, and let the syrup cool.

Transfer the plums to a food processor or blender, add
the cooled syrup and the egg white, and process to a
puree. Refrigerate for 3 hours.

Pour the mixture into an ice cream maker and churn for
about 30 minutes, or according to the manufacturer's
directions. Transfer the sorbet to the mold and freeze for
2–3 hours, until solid.

SORBETTO ALLA CILIEGIA
CHERRY SORBET

EASY

– Preparation time: *5 minutes
+ 3 hours chilling, 30 minutes
churning, and 2–3 hours
freezing*
– Calories per serving: *120*
– *Serves 4–6*

INGREDIENTS

– 2 cups (11 oz/300 g) ripe
cherries, pitted
– ¾ cup (5 oz/150 g) superfine
(caster) sugar
– ½ teaspoon almond extract
– 4–6 frozen cherries, to serve
(optional)

Put the cherries, sugar, and almond extract into a
blender, pour in scant 1 cup (7 fl oz/200 ml) water,
and blend to a puree. Refrigerate for hours.

Pour the mixture into an ice cream maker and churn
for about 30 minutes, or according to the manufacturer's
directions. Transfer the sorbet to the mold and freeze for
2–3 hours, until solid.

Serve with frozen cherries, if desired.

SORBETTO AL KIWI
KIWI SORBET

EASY

– Preparation time: *5 minutes
+ 3 hours chilling, 30 minutes
churning, and 2–3 hours
freezing*
– Cooking time: *15 minutes*
– Calories per serving: *240*
– *Serves 4*

INGREDIENTS

– 1 cup (7 oz/200 g) superfine
(caster) sugar
– 4 kiwi fruits, peeled and
coarsely chopped
– juice of 1 lemon, strained

Pour generous 2 cups (17 fl oz/500 ml) water into a heavy saucepan, add the sugar, and bring to a boil over low heat, stirring constantly, until the sugar has dissolved. Boil, without stirring, for 15 minutes, then remove from the heat.

Put the kiwis into a blender and process to a puree, then stir in the sugar syrup and lemon juice. Refrigerate for 3 hours.

Pour the mixture into an ice cream maker and churn for about 30 minutes, or according to the manufacturer's directions. Transfer the sorbet to a mold and freeze for 2–3 hours, until solid.

SORBETTO TROPICALE
TROPICAL SORBET

EASY

– Preparation time: *10 minutes
+ 3 hours chilling, 30 minutes
churning, and 2–3 hours
freezing*
– Calories per serving: *80*
– *Serves 4*

INGREDIENTS

– 1 egg white
– 2 tablespoons sugar
– 3 cups (25 fl oz/750 ml)
unsweetened mixed tropical
juice
– ⅓ cup (2½ fl oz/75 ml)
white dessert wine
– small mint leaves, to garnish

Whisk the egg white in a bowl or electric mixer to stiff peaks. Set aside.

In a bowl, dissolve the sugar in 2 tablespoons hot water, then add the fruit juice and stir. Add the wine, and fold the mixture gently into the egg white. Refrigerate for 3 hours.

Pour the mixture into an ice cream maker and churn for about 30 minutes, or according to the manufacturer's directions. Transfer the sorbet to a mold and freeze for 2–3 hours, until solid.

Divide the sorbet among glasses or small dishes and decorate with small mint leaves.

SORBETTO AL PROSECCO
PROSECCO SORBET

EASY

– Preparation time: *15 minutes
+ 3 hours chilling, 10 minutes
cooling, 30 minutes churning,
and 2–3 hours freezing*
– Cooking time: *5 minutes*
– Calories per serving: *126*
– *Serves 6*

INGREDIENTS

– 1¼ cups (9 oz/250 g) sugar
– juice of 2 lemons, strained
(sieved)
– generous 2 cups (17 fl oz/
500 ml) Prosecco (see Note)
or other dry sparkling white
wine
– 1 egg white

Pour scant 1 cup (7 fl oz/200 ml) water into a heavy
saucepan, add the sugar, and bring to a boil over low
heat, stirring until the sugar has dissolved. Remove
from the heat and gently stir in the lemon juice and the
Prosecco. Let cool.

Whisk the egg white in a bowl or electric mixer to stiff
peaks and fold it into the wine mixture. Refrigerate for
3 hours.

Pour the mixture into an ice cream maker and churn for
30 minutes or according to the manufacturer's directions.
Rinse a mold with cold water, then transfer the sorbet
into the mold and freeze for 2–3 hours, until solid.

Divide it among glasses and serve immediately, while it
is still cold.

*Note: Prosecco is a dry Italian sparkling white wine made
with Glera grapes.*

SORBETTO AL BASILICO
BASIL SORBET

EASY

– Preparation time: *30 minutes
+ 3 hours chilling, 30 minutes
churning, and 2–3 hours
freezing*
– Calories per serving: *206*
– *Serves 4*

INGREDIENTS

– generous 2 cups (17 fl oz/
500 ml) Prosecco or other
dry sparkling wine
– 16 basil leaves, plus extra to
decorate
– ½ cup (3½ oz/100 g) sugar
– juice of 1 lemon
– 4 egg whites

Put the sparkling wine, basil, sugar, and lemon juice into
a blender or food processor and process at maximum
speed for 1 minute. Strain (sieve) the pureed mixture
through a fine-mesh strainer (sieve).

Beat the egg whites in a bowl or electric mixer to stiff
peaks, then fold them gently into the wine mixture,
1 tablespoon at a time, and stirring as little as possible.
Refrigerate for 3 hours.

Pour the mixture into an ice cream maker and churn for
about 30 minutes, or according to the manufacturer's
directions. Rinse a mold with cold water, then transfer the
sorbet to the mold and freeze for 2–3 hours, until solid.

Remove the sorbet from the freezer, divide among
4 glasses or small dishes, decorate with a few whole
basil leaves, and serve.

FROZEN
DESSERTS

89   ICE CREAM CAKE WITH FRUIT

90   TRICOLOR ICE POPS

93   CAMPARI ICE POPS

94   GREYHOUND ICE POPS

97   PEACH GRANITA

98   RASPBERRY AND RED CURRANT
      GRANITA

101   COFFEE GRANITA WITH CREAM

102   ICED RASPBERRY AND
      STRAWBERRY SOUFFLÉ

105   ORANGES FILLED WITH ICE CREAM

106   MIXED FRUIT ICE CREAM

108   RASPBERRY SEMIFREDDO

111   MASCARPONE SEMIFREDDO

112   LADYFINGER DESSERT WITH
      APRICOT-FLAVORED BRANDY

115   CUSTARD AND CHOCOLATE
      SEMIFREDDO

116   PANFORTE AND SPICE BREAD
      SEMIFREDDO

119   ZABAGLIONE SEMIFREDDO

120   CHAMOMILE SEMIFREDDO

123   ALMOND BASKETS WITH
      STRAWBERRY ICE CREAM

124   ZUCCOTTO

STEP 1

STEP 2

STEP 3

STEP 4

TECHNIQUE

TORTA GELATO ALLA FRUTTA
ICE CREAM CAKE WITH FRUIT

EASY

– Preparation time: *20 minutes
+ 1 hour freezing*
– Calories per serving: *500*
– *Serves 8*

INGREDIENTS

– 3½ oz/100 g prepared
sponge cake, about
6½ inches/16 cm in diameter
– 11 oz/300 g rolled wafers
dipped in chocolate
– 4 cups (1 lb 2 oz/500 g)
Strawberry Ice Cream
(page 123)
– 1½ cups (7 oz/200 g) fior
di latte ice cream (see Note)
– 2 nectarines, pitted and
thinly sliced
– 4 apricots, pitted and thinly
sliced
– 4 strawberries, hulled and
halved
– 1 small sprig mint
– confectioners' (icing) sugar

STEP 1

Line a 7-inch/18-cm springform pan (tin) with parchment (baking) paper. Cut a 6½-inch/16-cm diameter disk out of the sponge cake and lay it at the bottom of the pan.

STEP 2

Arrange the rolled wafers upright against the edges of the pan, positioning their bottom ends in the small space between the cake and the side of the cake pan.

STEP 3

Use a spatula to cover the sponge cake with a layer of strawberry ice cream, followed by a layer of fior di latte ice cream, and top with a layer of strawberry ice cream.

STEP 4

Freeze the cake for at least 1 hour, unmold it carefully, discard the parchment (baking) paper, and transfer to a serving dish. Decorate with the sliced fruit, remaining wafers, and a few mint leaves. Dust with confectioners' (icing) sugar and serve.

Note: Fior di latte, *literally translated as "flower of milk," is a neutral, unflavored ice cream made without eggs.*

GHIACCIOLI TRICOLORE
TRICOLOR ICE POPS

AVERAGE

- Preparation time: *25 minutes*
  + 10 hours freezing
- Cooking time: *5 minutes*
- Calories per serving: *167*
- *Serves 4*

INGREDIENTS

- 2 kiwi, chopped
- 5 tablespoons sugar
- scant 1 cup (4½ oz/130 g)
  strawberries, hulled
- 1 ripe banana, mashed
- juice of ½ lemon

In a blender, combine the kiwi, 2 tablespoons sugar, and a little water, then blend to a puree. Transfer to a saucepan. Clean out the blender and repeat with the strawberries Clean out the blender and repeat with the strawberries, another 2 tablespoons sugar, a little water. Finally, clean out the blender, combine the banana, lemon juice, 1 tablespoon sugar, and 1 tablespoon water and blend to a puree.

Cook each puree separately over low heat for 5 minutes, then remove from the heat and pour the kiwi puree into ice pop (lolly) molds. Freeze for 2 hours.

Take the molds out of the freezer and add a layer of the banana puree to each mold, then return to the freezer for another 2 hours.

Take the molds out of the freezer again and add a layer of strawberry puree in each mold, then insert the sticks. Return to the freezer for another 6 hours, or until solid.

Tip: Prepare each layer at separate times, right before freezing. Alternatively, prepare them at the same time but store the strawberry and banana purees in the refrigerator while the other layers freeze.

GHIACCIOLI AL CAMPARI

CAMPARI ICE POPS

EASY

– Preparation time: *15 minutes*
  + 12 hours freezing
– Cooking time: *10 minutes*
– Calories per serving: *160*
– *Serves 6*

INGREDIENTS

– ⅔ cup (11½ oz/325 g)
  superfine (caster) sugar
– scant 1 cup (7 fl oz/200 ml)
  blood orange juice
– 3 tablespoons Campari

Put 1½ cups (12 fl oz/350 ml) water and the sugar into a small saucepan, place over medium heat, and boil for 7 minutes. Remove from the heat and let cool.

When the mixture is cold, stir in the blood orange juice and the Campari thoroughly. Fill ice pop (lolly) molds two-thirds full, insert the sticks, and freeze for 12 hours, or until solid. Take out and serve immediately.

GHIACCIOLI "SPIRITOSI"

GREYHOUND ICE POPS

EASY

– Preparation time: *15 minutes*
  + 12 hours freezing
– Cooking time: *10 minutes*
– Calories per serving: *155*
– *Serves 4*

INGREDIENTS

– 1 cup (200 g/7 oz) superfine
  (caster) sugar
– ⅔ cup (150 ml/5 fl oz)
  grapefruit juice
– 2 tablespoons vodka

Pour 1 cup (8 fl oz/250 ml) water into a small saucepan, add the sugar, place over medium heat, and boil for 5 minutes. Remove from the heat and let cool.

Add the grapefruit juice and vodka to the cooled mixture, then divide the mixture among the ice pop (lolly) molds, and insert ice pop sticks into the hole in each mold. Freeze for 12 hours, or until solid.

GRANITA ALLA PESCA
PEACH GRANITA

EASY

- Preparation time: *15 minutes*
  + 20 minutes cooling and
  3 hours freezing
- Cooking time: *40 minutes*
- Calories per serving: *180*
- *Serves 4*

INGREDIENTS

- ¾ cup (5 oz/150 g) superfine
  (caster) sugar
- 3 peaches, peeled, pitted,
  and diced
- juice of 1 lemon, strained
- 1 teaspoon vanilla extract
- 4 thick lemon slices, to
  decorate (optional)

In a heavy saucepan, combine the sugar and a scant
1 cup (7 fl oz/200 ml) water, and bring to a boil, stirring
until the sugar has dissolved. Boil over low heat, without
stirring, for about 10 minutes, until syrupy. Remove from
the heat and let cool.

Add the peaches to the cooled syrup, cover with a lid, and
cook over medium heat for 30 minutes. Remove from the
heat and let cool.

Rub the mixture through a nylon strainer (sieve) into a
bowl and stir in the lemon juice and vanilla extract. Pour
the mixture into a freezer-proof container and freeze,
stirring every 30 minutes, using a fork to break up the
crystals, for at least 3 hours.

Remove from the freezer and divide the granita among
4 glasses. Decorate with lemon slices, if using, and serve.

GRANITA AL LAMPONE E RIBES
RASPBERRY AND RED CURRANT GRANITA

EASY

– Preparation time: *20 minutes*
  + 3 hours freezing
– Cooking time: *10 minutes*
– Calories per serving: *160*
– *Serves 4*

INGREDIENTS

– 1 cup (6½ oz/185 g)
  raspberries
– 1¼ cups (5 oz/140 g) red
  currants
– ½ cup (3½ oz/100 g)
  superfine (caster) sugar
– juice of ½ lemon, strained

Push the raspberries and red currants through a nylon strainer (sieve) into a bowl and set aside.

In a heavy saucepan, combine the sugar and a scant 1 cup (7 fl oz/200 ml) water, and bring to a boil, stirring until the sugar has dissolved. Boil over low heat, without stirring, for 5 minutes, until the mixture is syrupy. Remove from the heat and let cool.

Stir the fruit puree and lemon juice into the cooled syrup, then pour the mixture into a freezer-proof container and freeze, stirring every 30 minutes using a fork to break up the crystals, for 3 hours.

Remove the granita from the freezer and divide among individual glass bowls.

Tip: You can use strawberries or blueberries if red currants are not available.

GRANITA AL CAFFÈ CON PANNA

COFFEE GRANITA WITH CREAM

EASY

– Preparation time: *10 minutes
+ 2 hours freezing*
– Cooking time: *5 minutes*
– Calories per serving: *150*
– *Serves 4*

INGREDIENTS

– scant ⅔ cup (4 oz/120 g)
superfine (caster) sugar
– scant 1 cup (7 fl oz/200 ml)
cold coffee
– 1¼ cups (10 fl oz/300 ml)
heavy (double) cream,
whipped
– ¼ cup (1 oz/30 g)
confectioners' (icing) sugar
– cocoa powder, for dusting

Pour a generous 2 cups (17 fl oz/500 ml) of water into a heavy saucepan, add the sugar, and bring to a boil, stirring until the sugar has dissolved. Boil over low heat, without stirring, for 2–3 minutes, then remove from the heat and let cool.

Add the coffee to the syrup, stir, then pour into a deep container, cover with a lid, and freeze for 1 hour, or until the edges are frozen. Remove and stir using a fork to break up the crystals, then freeze, stirring every 30 minutes, for 2 hours, until it is completely solid.

Mix the whipped cream and confectioners' (icing) sugar together. Divide the granita among 4 glasses and top with whipped cream. Dust with cocoa powder and serve.

Tip: You can flavor the syrup with 2–3 green cardamom pods, or the grated zest of an unwaxed bitter orange, or with a vanilla bean (pod), slit lengthwise.

SOUFFLÉ GELATO AL LAMPONE E FRAGOLA

ICED RASPBERRY AND STRAWBERRY SOUFFLÉ

AVERAGE

– Preparation time: *20 minutes*
  + 3 hours freezing
– Cooking time: *5 minutes*
– Calories per serving: *740*
– *Serves 4*

INGREDIENTS

– generous 1 cup (5 oz/140 g)
  raspberries, plus extra to
  decorate
– 1¾ cups (9 oz/250 g) hulled
  strawberries
– 1 cup (7 oz/200 g) superfine
  (caster) sugar
– 5 teaspoons strawberry
  liqueur, or other fruit
  liqueur
– grated zest of ½ lemon
– generous 2 cups (17 fl oz/
  500 ml) heavy (double)
  cream
– 3 leaves gelatin

Cut a 2¼-inch/6-cm strip of wax (greaseproof) paper to fit the circumference of a soufflé dish. Use adhesive tape to attach the paper around the rim of the dish, which creates a little collar.

Put the raspberries and strawberries into a blender, add the sugar, liqueur, and zest, and blend until smooth and frothy. Pour the mixture into a bowl and set aside.

Whip the cream in a bowl or electric mixer to stiff peaks.

Put the gelatin into a heatproof bowl and pour in enough cold water to cover. Set the bowl over a saucepan of barely simmering water and heat over low heat for 3–4 minutes until the gelatin has dissolved. Cool slightly, then add the whipped cream and gelatin to the berry mixture. Fold in, being careful not to knock the air out of the mixture.

Pour the mixture into the prepared dish and freeze for 3 hours. To serve, remove the paper from the dish and decorate the soufflé with raspberries.

ARANCE RIPIENE DI GELATO
ORANGES FILLED WITH ICE CREAM

EASY

– Preparation time: *20 minutes*
– Cooking time: *5 minutes*
– Calories per serving: *200*
– *Serves 4*

INGREDIENTS

– 4 large oranges
– 2 tablespoons orange-
flavored liqueur
– 2 tablespoons unsalted
pistachios nuts, coarsely
chopped
– 2 cups (11 oz/300 g) orange
or lemon ice cream

Cut off the top part of the oranges to form a lid and set aside, then scoop out the flesh with a grapefruit knife or small serrated knife, without piercing the peel. Finely dice the flesh, put into a bowl, add the liqueur, and stir to mix. Sprinkle with the chopped pistachio nuts.

Arrange the orange mixture in the prepared orange containers, fill with ice cream, and top with the lid (optional).

Tip: After filling the oranges with the ice cream, you can top them with meringue, made by whisking 2 egg whites stiffly with ¾ cup (5 oz/150 g) superfine (caster) sugar and brown lightly with a chef's torch or under the broiler (grill).

PACIUGO®

MIXED FRUIT ICE CREAM

EASY

– Preparation time: *10 minutes*
– Calories per serving: *436*
– *Serves 4*

INGREDIENTS

– 2 cups (9 oz/250 g) vanilla
  ice cream
– scant 1 cup (7 fl oz/
  200 ml) heavy (double)
  cream, whipped
– ⅔ cup (3½ oz/100 g)
  strawberries in syrup,
  drained and chopped
– 2 cups (9 oz/250 g)
  Strawberry Ice Cream
  (see page 42)
– 4 tablespoons grenadine
  syrup

Put a layer of vanilla ice cream ¾ inch/2 cm high in the bottom of 4 glasses, and top with a layer of the whipped cream, then sprinkle with a few chopped, drained strawberries. Cover these with a layer of strawberry ice cream and lay a few more strawberries in syrup on top. Finish with a generous swirl of whipped cream, then carefully drizzle with the grenadine syrup drawing a few swirls. Serve immediately.

Tip: This mixed ice cream is best served in fairly tall, cylindrical glasses, which should be kept in the freezer for a few hours before eating. When you are ready to serve, whip the cream in a bowl or electric mixer to soft peaks.

SEMIFREDDO AL LAMPONE
RASPBERRY SEMIFREDDO

EASY

– Preparation time: *30 minutes*
  + 4 hours freezing
– Cooking time: *20 minutes*
– Calories per serving: *692–519*
– *Serves 6–8*

INGREDIENTS

– 3 cups (25 fl oz/750 ml)
  heavy (double) cream
– 2 cups (9 oz/250 g)
  raspberries, plus extra to
  decorate
– 6 egg yolks
– 1¼ cups (9 oz/250 g)
  superfine (caster) sugar

Line an 8 × 4-inch (20 × 10-cm) loaf pan (tin) with plastic wrap (clingfilm) with the sides overhanging. Whip the cream in a bowl or electric mixer to soft peaks. In a small bowl, crush the raspberries with the tines of a fork and set aside.

Gently whisk the egg yolks with the sugar in a double boiler or in a heatproof bowl set over a saucepan of barely simmering water until pale and frothy. Cook, whisking constantly, until the mixture has thickened and forms a ribbon when the whisk is lifted above the saucepan. Remove from the heat and whisk until the custard has completely cooled.

Gently fold the whipped cream into the custard, then add the crushed raspberries. Pour the mixture into the lined loaf pan, smooth the top, and cover with the remaining plastic wrap. Freeze for at least 4 hours, or until solid.

Unmold the frozen mousse onto a serving dish and remove the plastic wrap without damaging the surface of the dessert. Cut it into ¼-inch/½-cm-thick slices and decorate with raspberries.

Tip: To cut the frozen mousse easily, dip a knife in hot water each time you slice. Add the whipped cream to the egg yolk-and-sugar mixture only when cool to avoid letting the cream become too runny.

SEMIFREDDO AL MASCARPONE
MASCARPONE SEMIFREDDO

EASY

– Preparation time: *30 minutes
  + 2 hours freezing*
– Calories per serving: *373*
– *Serves 6*

INGREDIENTS

– 3⅓ sheets gelatin
– 1 tablespoon hot cream or
  milk
– 3 eggs, separated
– generous ¾ cup (3½ oz/
  100 g) confectioners' (icing)
  sugar
– 1⅓ cups (11 oz/300 g)
  mascarpone cheese
– 2 oz/50 g semisweet (plain)
  chocolate, chopped
– 1 teaspoon instant coffee,
  finely powdered
– chocolate leaves, to decorate

In a small bowl, combine the gelatin with cold water and soak for 5 minutes, or until softened. Drain, then combine with the hot cream and stir until dissolved.

Line an 8 × 4-inch (20 × 10-cm) loaf pan (tin) with plastic wrap (clingfilm) with the sides overhanging. Using an electric mixer, beat the egg whites to stiff peaks in a grease-free bowl.

In a separate bowl, beat the egg yolks with the sugar until pale and frothy. Add the mascarpone cheese, chocolate, instant coffee powder, and whipped egg whites and gently stir until everything is mixed together.

Pour the mixture into the lined pan, cover with the plastic wrap, and freeze for 2 hours, or until solid.

Remove from the freezer, unmold onto a serving dish, remove and discard the plastic wrap, decorate with chocolate leaves, and serve.

MATTONELLA DI SAVOIARDI ALL'APRICOT

LADYFINGER DESSERT WITH APRICOT-FLAVORED BRANDY

EASY

– Preparation time: *25 minutes + 6 hours freezing*
– Calories per serving: *531*
– *Serves 4*

INGREDIENTS

– 8 ladyfingers (sponge fingers)
– scant ¼–½ cup (2–4 fl oz/ 50–120 ml) apricot-flavored brandy
– generous ¾ cup (3 oz/80 g) finely chopped almonds
– 1½ cups (7 oz/200 g) Chocolate Ice Cream (see page 19)
– 1½ cups (7 oz/200 g) Egg Custard Ice Cream (see page 19)
– scant ½ cup (2 oz/50 g) unsweetened cocoa powder, sifted

Soak the ladyfingers (sponge fingers) in the apricot-flavored brandy.

Carefully stir the almonds into the chocolate ice cream to distribute them evenly. Pour the ice cream into an 8 × 4-inch (20 × 10-cm) mold, and smooth the top with a wet spoon.

Arrange a layer of the soaked ladyfingers on the chocolate ice cream and top with a layer of the custard ice cream, smoothing the top again with a wet spoon. Cover with a sheet of wax (greaseproof) paper or parchment (baking) paper and freeze for 6 hours, or until solid.

Remove the dessert from the freezer, rest at room temperature for 10 minutes, then unmold onto a serving dish discarding the wax or parchment paper. Dust the top with sifted cocoa and serve.

Tip: Alternatively, use 3 oz/80 g crushed almond praline instead of the skinned almonds and stir ¼ cup (3 oz/80 g) finely chopped candied orange peel into the custard ice cream.

SEMIFREDDO ALLA CREMA E CIOCCOLATO

CUSTARD AND CHOCOLATE SEMIFREDDO

EASY

– Preparation time: *20 minutes*
  + 40 minutes cooling and
  12 hours freezing
– Cooking time: *20 minutes*
– Calories per serving: *318–238*
– *Serves 6–8*

INGREDIENTS

– 1 cup (8 fl oz/250 ml) milk
– 3 egg yolks
– ½ cup (3½ oz/100 g)
  superfine (caster) sugar
– 2 tablespoons (½ oz/15 g)
  all-purpose (plain) flour
– ⅓ cup (1¼ oz/30 g)
  unsweetened cocoa powder
– generous 2 cups (17 fl oz/
  500 ml) heavy (double)
  cream
– 1 tablespoon vanilla sugar
  (see page 41)

Line an 8 × 4-inch (20 × 10-cm) mold with plastic wrap (clingfilm) with the sides overhanging. Set aside 2–3 tablespoons of the milk, pour the rest into a saucepan, and bring to a simmer.

Whisk the egg yolks and sugar in a heavy saucepan. While stirring, gradually add the flour and hot milk and simmer for 4 minutes, stirring constantly.

Pour the mixture into a bowl and let cool, stirring frequently so it does not form a skin on the top. Pour half of the mixture into a heavy saucepan, add the cocoa and the remaining milk, and cook for 3–4 minutes. Remove from the heat and let cool, then chill both mixtures in the refrigerator. (To prevent the hot custard from forming a skin on top, place a piece of plastic wrap on the surface.)

Using an electric mixture, whip the cream and the vanilla sugar in a bowl, then divide in half and add to both cooled mixtures. Pour half of the cocoa mixture into the lined mold, pour the other mixture on top, and then finish with the remaining cocoa mixture. Cover with the remaining plastic wrap and freeze for 12 hours, or until solid.

SEMIFREDDO AL PANFORTE E PAN DI SPEZIE

PANFORTE AND SPICE BREAD SEMIFREDDO

EASY

– Preparation time: *30 minutes*
  + 24 hours freezing
– Cooking time: *40 minutes*
– Calories per serving: *493*
– *Serves 12*

INGREDIENTS

– 3½ oz/100 g spice bread,
  finely chopped
– ⅔ cup (5 fl oz/150 ml) milk
– 2 eggs, separated
– scant ¼ cup (1½ oz/40 g)
  granulated sugar
– 5 oz/150 g panforte, finely
  chopped
– scant ⅔ cup (2¾ oz/70 g)
  confectioners' (icing) sugar
– 1⅔ cups (14 fl oz/400 ml)
  heavy (double) cream,
  whipped
– 2 oz/50 g semisweet (plain)
  chocolate shavings, to
  decorate

FOR THE SAUCE

– generous 2 cups (17 fl oz/
  500 ml) milk
– 8 egg yolks
– ⅔ cup (4½ oz/130 g) sugar
– generous pinch of potato
  flour
– 2 tablespoons Grand Marnier
– 3 tablespoons chopped
  candied orange peel

Line an 8 × 4-inch (20 × 10-cm) mold with plastic wrap (clingfilm) with the sides overhanging.

Soak the spice bread in ½ cup (3½ fl oz/100 ml) of milk. In a saucepan, bring the remaining milk to a boil.

Using an electric mixer, whisk the egg whites to stiff peaks in a separate grease-free bowl.

Whisk the egg yolks with the granulated sugar in the top half of a double boiler or a heatproof bowl, then add the remaining hot milk. Place over a double boiler or pan of barely simmering water until the custard reaches a temperature of 167°F/75°C.

Pour the mixture into a bowl, add the panforte and the spice bread, then fold in the whipped egg whites, confectioners' (icing) sugar, and whipped cream. Pour the mixture into the lined mold, cover with the remaining plastic wrap, and freeze for at least 24 hours.

Make the sauce. Bring the milk to a boil in a saucepan. Whisk the egg yolks in a double boiler or a heatproof bowl set over a saucepan of barely simmering water with the sugar and potato flour. While stirring, drizzle in the hot milk and cook the mixture, stirring constantly, until it reaches a temperature of 185°F/85°C. Add the Grand Marnier and candied peel, stir, and let the sauce cool.

Unmold the dessert, then remove and discard the plastic wrap. Slice the semifreddo and drizzle with the sauce. Decorate with chocolate shaving and serve.

Note: Panforte is a traditional Italian cake-like dessert made with fruit and nuts, available at gourmet Italian stores. It can be substituted with a fruitcake, if needed.

SEMIFREDDO ALLO ZABAIONE

ZABAGLIONE SEMIFREDDO

AVERAGE

– Preparation time: *30 minutes
  + 6 hours freezing*
– Cooking time: *1 hour*
– Calories per serving: *677–451*
– *Serves 4–6*

INGREDIENTS

– 4 egg yolks
– scant ⅔ cup (4 oz/120 g)
  superfine (caster) sugar
– ½ cup (4 fl oz/120 ml)
  Marsala or dry white wine
– 1⅔ cups (14 fl oz/400 ml)
  heavy (double) cream
– 1 vanilla bean (pod), split in
  half lengthwise (optional)

TO DECORATE

– strawberries, hulled and
  halved
– 2 apricots, pitted and halved
  (optional)

Line a round 7-inch/18-cm springform pan (tin) with plastic wrap (clingfilm) with the sides overhanging.

Beat the egg yolks with the sugar in a large double boiler or in a heatproof bowl set over a saucepan of barely simmering water until pale and frothy. Then, while stirring, gradually add the Marsala or wine and cook over low heat for about 10 minutes, stirring constantly, (do not let the mixture boil), until it has increased considerably in volume. Remove from the heat and let cool.

Scrape the seeds from the vanilla bean (pod) and add it to a large bowl. Add the cream and whip to stiff peaks. Fold it into the cold zabaglione, gently stirring from the top to the bottom. Pour the mixture into the lined loaf pan, smooth the top, cover with the remaining plastic wrap, and freeze for 6 hours.

Unmold the semifreddo, remove and discard the plastic wrap, decorate with the strawberries and apricots, if using.

SEMIFREDDO ALLA CAMOMILLA
CHAMOMILE SEMIFREDDO

– Preparation time: *30 minutes*
  + 20 minutes cooling and
  4 hours freezing
– Cooking time: *10 minutes*
– Calories per serving: *360*
– *Serves 4*

INGREDIENTS

– 7 oz/200 g fresh unsprayed
  chamomile flowers
– ½ cup (3½ oz/100 g)
  superfine (caster) sugar
– 3 eggs, separated
– 4 tablespoons sweet Marsala
  or dry white wine
– juice of ½ lemon, strained
– scant 1 cup (7 fl oz/200 ml)
  heavy (double) cream
– chopped almonds, to
  decorate

Line an 8 × 4-inch (20 × 10-cm) loaf pan (tin) with plastic wrap (clingfilm) with the sides overhanging.

Put the chamomile flowers and sugar into a large saucepan, pour in scant 1 cup (7 fl oz/200 ml) water, and bring to a boil, stirring, until the sugar has dissolved. Boil, without stirring, until a thick syrup forms. Pour the syrup through a fine strainer (sieve) into a bowl, lightly pressing the flowers to extract the liquid, then let cool.

Beat the egg yolks into the cooled chamomile syrup until thickened, then add the Marsala and lemon juice.

Whisk the egg whites in a grease-free bowl or electric mixer to stiff peaks. In another bowl or electric mixer, whip the cream to stiff peaks. Fold the egg whites into the chamomile mixture, then fold in the cream.
Pour the mixture into the lined container, smooth the top, cover with the remaining plastic wrap, and freeze for 4 hours, or until frozen.

Sprinkle with chopped almonds to decorate and serve.

CESTINI DI MANDORLE CON GELATO ALLA FRAGOLA

ALMOND BASKETS WITH STRAWBERRY ICE CREAM

EASY

– Preparation time: *30 minutes
+ 4 hours chilling, 30 minutes
churning, and 3 hours freezing*
– Cooking time: *20 minutes*
– Calories per serving: *261*
– *Serves 6*

FOR THE ICE CREAM

– scant ¼ cup (1¾ fl oz/50 ml)
heavy (double) cream
– ½ cup (2¼ oz/65 g)
strawberries
– scant ¼ cup (1½ oz/45 g)
superfine (caster) sugar
– 5 tablespoons milk

FOR THE ALMOND BASKETS

– generous ¼ cup (2¼ oz/
60 g) superfine (caster) sugar
– 2 tablespoons (1 oz/25 g)
butter
– 1 tablespoon (¾ oz/20 g)
honey
– ¼ cup (1 oz/30 g) all-purpose
(plain) flour
– scant ½ cup (1½ oz/40 g)
ground almonds (almond
meal)

TO DECORATE

– whipped cream
– wild strawberries, hulled and
quartered

To make the ice cream, whip the cream in a bowl or an electric mixer to soft peaks. Put the strawberries, sugar, and milk into a blender and process, then add the whipped cream. Refrigerate for 4 hours.

Pour the mixture into an ice cream maker and churn for about 30 minutes, or according to the manufacturer's directions. Transfer the ice cream into a mold and freeze for about 3 hours, until solid.

Preheat the oven to 400°F/200°C/Gas Mark 6.

To make into the almond baskets, put the sugar, butter, and honey in a heavy saucepan, place over low heat, and cook for 5 minutes, stirring constantly. Remove from the heat and carefully stir in the flour and almonds.

Line a baking sheet with parchment (baking) paper and spoon the mixture onto it to form 6 thin disks. Cook in the hot oven for 15 minutes, or until the disks are golden brown. Remove and while still hot and malleable, mold them around the bottom of an upturned glass into cup shapes. Let dry.

Arrange the almond baskets on 6 dessert plates, fill them with 3 scoops of ice cream, and decorate with a little whipped cream and a few wild strawberries. Serve.

ZUCCOTTO
ZUCCOTTO

ZUCCOTTO

EASY

– Preparation time: *30 minutes*
  + 6 hours freezing
– Calories per serving: *660*
– *Serves 6*

INGREDIENTS

– 1 (9–11-oz/250–300-g) pan
  di Spagna, pound cake, or
  Madeira cake
– ½ cup (4 fl oz/120 ml)
  amaretto liqueur
– generous 2 cups (17 fl oz/
  500 ml) heavy (double)
  cream
– generous ⅓ cup (3 oz/80 g)
  superfine (caster) sugar
– ⅔ cup (2 oz/60 g)
  unsweetened cocoa powder
– 4 amaretti cookies (biscuits)

Line a freezer-proof bombe mold with plastic wrap (clingfilm). Cut the cake horizontally into 2 circles of equal thickness. Divide one of the circles into 8 wedges and use to line the bottom and sides of the mold. Mix the liqueur with a little water and sprinkle it over the cake slices.

Whip the cream in a bowl or electric mixer to stiff peaks, gradually adding the sugar. Spoon half of the cream into another bowl and fold in half the unsweetened cocoa powder. Crumble the amaretti into the remaining cream and spoon into the mold, gently spreading it over the side and leaving a small hollow in the center. Spoon the cocoa cream into the hollow and smooth the surface. Put the remaining cake circle on top, cover with plastic wrap, and freeze for at least 6 hours.

Turn out the zuccotto onto a serving dish and remove and discard the plastic wrap. Dust the remaining unsweetened cocoa powder over the dessert and serve immediately.

Note: According to legend, zuccotto is the first semifreddo in the history of cooking and was originally made in an infantryman's studded helmet. In the Tuscan dialect, zucca *means "head." It was originally prepared with ricotta, candied (glacé) fruit, almonds, and semisweet (plain) chocolate.*

CHILLED DESSERTS

129   FRUIT SALAD WITH ICE CREAM

130   MELON BALLS WITH MINT-FLAVORED YOGURT

133   PLUMS WITH ICE CREAM

134   AVOCADO, YOGURT, AND HONEY CREAM

137   FIGS WITH CREAM

138   MELON AND WATERMELON ASPIC

141   RICOTTA AND APRICOT CREAM

142   ORANGE CUPS WITH CREAM

145   FRUITS OF THE FOREST BAVAROIS

146   CHILLED WATERMELON

149   MELON SURPRISE

150   PEACH ASPIC

153   CHILLED WINE WITH STRAWBERRIES

154   CANNOLI

157   WINE BAVAROIS

158   FRUIT GELATIN

161   PANNA COTTA

162   TIRAMISU

165   FRUIT IN SPARKLING WINE

166   ITALIAN TRIFLE

169   AMARETTI CHARLOTTE

170   SICILIAN CASSATA

173   FRUITS OF THE FOREST CHARLOTTE

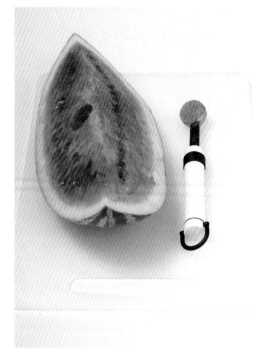

TECHNIQUE

MACEDONIA CON GELATO
FRUIT SALAD WITH ICE CREAM

EASY

- Preparation time: *15 minutes*
  + 10 minutes cooling
- Cooking time: *5 minutes*
- Calories per serving: *250*
- *Serves 6*

INGREDIENTS

- 1¼ cups (5 oz/150 g)
  raspberries
- ¼ cup (2 oz/50 g) superfine
  (caster) sugar
- juice of 1 lemon
- ¼ watermelon
- 1 bunch red seedless grapes,
  halved
- 3 apricots, pitted and sliced
- generous ¾ cup (4 oz/120 g)
  blueberries
- 2 white nectarines, pitted
  and sliced
- 2 cups (11 oz/300 g) Egg
  Custard Ice Cream (see
  page 19)
- 1 small sprig mint

STEP 1

In a heavy saucepan, combine the raspberries, sugar, and lemon juice, bring to a boil, and cook for 2–3 minutes, then let cool. Puree the raspberries with an immersion (stick) blender, then strain (sieve) the fruit through a fine-mesh strainer (sieve). Set aside.

STEP 2

Remove and discard the seeds in the watermelon, then scoop out the flesh into small balls with a melon baller.

STEP 3

In a bowl, add the watermelon balls, grapes, apricots, blueberries, and nectarines. Add the raspberry sauce and stir to mix.

STEP 4

Divide the fruit salad among 4 bowls, top with the ice cream, and decorate with mint leaves.

Tip: Instead of the raspberry sauce, you could flavor the fruit salad with a syrup made with ¼ cup (2 oz/50 g) sugar, a scant ½ cup (3½ fl oz/100 ml) water, and a large handful of mint leaves. Boil for 1 minute, let stand for 10 minutes so the flavors mingle, and strain (sieve).

PALLINE DI MELONE CON YOGURT ALLA MENTA

MELON BALLS WITH MINT-FLAVORED YOGURT

EASY

– Preparation time: 10 minutes
  + *2–3 hours chilling*
– Calories per serving: *120–90*
– *Serves 6–8*

INGREDIENTS

– 2 cups (1 lb/450 g) Greek-
  style yogurt
– 4 teaspoons clear honey
– 2 sprigs mint, chopped
– 2 melons

Mix together the yogurt, honey, and mint in a bowl, then let stand in the refrigerator for 2–3 hours.

Halve the melons, remove and discard the seeds, and scoop out as many balls of the flesh as possible with a melon baller.

Mix the melon balls with the yogurt sauce and pour the mixture into a large glass bowl. Chill in the refrigerator for 10 minutes before serving.

PRUGNE CON GELATO

PLUMS WITH ICE CREAM

EASY

– Preparation time: *15 minutes*
– Cooking time: *20 minutes*
– Calories per serving: *529*
– *Serves 4*

INGREDIENTS

– 8 plums
– 1 teaspoon vanilla sugar
  (see page 41)
– ½ cup (4 fl oz/120 ml) heavy
  (double) cream
– 1 teaspoon confectioners'
  (icing) sugar
– Banana Ice Cream (see page
  22) or Zabaglione ice cream
  (see page 57)
– small cherries, to decorate
  (optional)

Bring a saucepan of water to a boil. Carefully lower the plums into the boiling water and blanch for 2–3 minutes, then remove them from the pan and carefully peel off the skins. Cut the plums in half and remove the pits (stones). Put the plums into a saucepan, sprinkle with the vanilla sugar, stir, and cook briefly until the sugar has dissolved.

Meanwhile, whip the cream in a bowl or electric mixer, then sweeten with the confectioners' (icing) sugar and use it to fill a pastry (piping) bag.

Place a few scoops of banana or zabaglione ice cream in the bottom of 4 glasses, add the plums on top, and top with whipped cream. Add a small cherry, if desired, to each glass.

CREMA DI YOGURT AL MIELE E AVOCADO

AVOCADO, YOGURT, AND HONEY CREAM

– Preparation time: *25 minutes*
– Cooking time: *10 minutes*
– Calories per serving: *300*
– *Serves 4*

INGREDIENTS

– ⅔ cup (3½ oz/100 g) shelled hazelnuts
– 1 cup (8 oz/225 g) yogurt
– scant ¼ cup (2 oz/50 g) honey
– 1 ripe avocado

Preheat the oven to 325°F/160°C/Gas Mark 3.

Spread out the hazelnuts on a baking sheet and toast in the oven for 10 minutes. Remove from the oven and transfer to a clean dish towel. Rub off the skins with the dish towel, then put the hazelnuts into a food processor and chop.

Mix the yogurt and honey together in a bowl. Peel and halve the avocado, remove and discard the pit (stone), then dice the flesh and add it to the yogurt mixture to prevent discoloration. Stir gently, then transfer to a glass bowl and sprinkle with the chopped hazelnuts. Chill until ready to serve.

FICHI ALLA CREMA
FIGS WITH CREAM

EASY

– Preparation time: *30 minutes*
  + 2 hours chilling
– Calories per serving: *300*
– *Serves 4*

INGREDIENTS

– 8 figs
– scant ¼ cup (1½ oz/40 g)
  superfine (caster) sugar
– rum, for drizzling
– scant 1 cup (7 fl oz/200 ml)
  heavy (double) cream

Peel the figs, being careful not to break them up. Make a series of cuts almost all the way through each fig to create a star shape and put them into a dish. Sprinkle with the sugar, drizzle with rum, and chill in the refrigerator for 2 hours.

Using an electric mixer, whip the cream to stiff peaks in a bowl. Using a slotted spoon, transfer the figs to a round serving dish. Put spoonfuls of cream in the middle of each and spoon a little of their juices on top.

ASPIC DI ANGURIA E MELONE
MELON AND WATERMELON ASPIC

AVERAGE

– Preparation time: *30 minutes
+ 10 hours chilling*
– Cooking time: *25 minutes*
– Calories per serving: *580*
– *Serves 8*

INGREDIENTS

– 2 small watermelons, halved
and seeds discarded
– 4 cantaloupe melons, halved
and seeds discarded

FOR THE SYRUP

– 2 ½ oz (65 g) leaves gelatin
– 1 cup (14 oz/200 g)
superfine (caster) sugar

**FOR THE SAUCE
(OPTIONAL)**

– ½ cantaloupe melon, seeded
– 1 cup (7 oz/200 g) superfine
(caster) sugar
– ½ cup (4 fl oz/120 ml)
Prosecco or other sparkling
wine

Put the watermelon flesh into a food processor or blender and process to a puree, then transfer to a bowl.

Put the cantaloupe melon flesh in a food processor or blender and process to a puree, then transfer to a separate bowl. Set aside.

To make the syrup, put the gelatin sheets into a bowl of cold water and let stand for 5 minutes to soften. Pour 3½ cups (27 fl oz/800 ml) water into a saucepan, stir in the sugar, and cook over medium heat, stirring constantly, until all the sugar has dissolved. Boil, without stirring, for 5 minutes, then squeeze out the gelatin and mix it into the syrup.

Divide the syrup between the bowls of melon puree, mixing it in well. Pour half the cantaloupe mixture into a large gelatin (jelly) mold and chill in the refrigerator for about 1 hour, or until it is just set.

Add the watermelon mixture to the mold, return to the refrigerator, and chill for about 1 hour, or until it is just set. Add the remaining cantaloupe mixture to the mold, return to the refrigerator, and chill overnight until completely set.

To make the sauce, put the melon flesh into a food processor or blender, and process to a puree. Pass the puree through a strainer (sieve) into a bowl. Pour a scant 1 cup (7 fl oz/200 ml) water into a saucepan, add the sugar, and bring to a boil, stirring until the sugar has dissolved. Boil, without stirring, until the mixture has turned a light golden color, then remove from the heat and stir in the sparkling wine and half the melon puree. Serve with the melon.

CREMA ALLA RICOTTA E ALBICOCCHE
RICOTTA AND APRICOT CREAM

EASY

– Preparation time: *10 minutes*
– Calories per serving: *320*
– *Serves 4*

INGREDIENTS

– scant 1 cup (7 oz/200 g)
  ricotta cheese
– 4 tablespoons vanilla sugar
  (see page 41)
– ½ cup (5 oz/140 g) apricot
  preserves or jam
– scant ½ cup (3½ fl oz/
  100 ml) heavy (double)
  cream

Beat the ricotta, sugar, and preserves together in a bowl.

Whip the cream in another bowl or electric mixer to stiff peaks, then fold it into the ricotta mixture. Divide the mixture among 4 individual dishes and chill in the refrigerator until ready to serve.

CESTINI DI ARANCE CON CREMA
ORANGE CUPS WITH CREAM

AVERAGE

– Preparation time: *1 hours +
20 minutes cooling and 3 hours
chilling*
– Cooking time: *25 minutes*
– Calories per serving: *300*
– *Serves 4*

INGREDIENTS

– 4 oranges
– ⅔–1 cup (5–8 fl oz/
150–250 ml) milk
– 3 egg yolks
– ⅔ cup (4½ oz/130 g)
superfine (caster) sugar
– ⅓ cup (1½ oz/40 g) all-
purpose (plain) flour
– 2 tablespoons orange liqueur

Cut a slice off the tops of the oranges and scoop out the flesh and juice into a bowl with a teaspoon. Set aside the cups. Put the flesh and juice into a strainer (sieve) set over a liquid measuring cup (jug) and extract from it as much liquid as possible by pressing down with the back of a spoon. Add enough milk so that there is generous 2 cups (17 fl oz/500 ml) liquid.

Beat the egg yolks and sugar together in a bowl until pale and fluffy, then sift the flour over the bowl and fold into the eggs. Gradually, stir in the orange juice mixture, then pour the mixture into a saucepan and cook over low heat, stirring constantly with a wooden spoon, for 20–25 minutes, or until the mixture is thick enough to coat the back of the spoon.

Remove the pan from the heat and let cool. Stir the liqueur into the mixture and divide it among the orange cups. Cover with plastic wrap (clingfilm) and chill in the refrigerator for about 3 hours, or until set.

BAVARESE AI FRUTTI DI BOSCO
FRUITS OF THE FOREST BAVAROIS

AVERAGE

– Preparation time: *45 minutes*
  + 6–8 hours chilling
– Calories per serving: *390*
– *Serves 8*

INGREDIENTS

– 7 sheets gelatin
– 1¾ cups (5 oz/150 g) wild
  strawberries
– 3½ cups (1 lb 2 oz/500 g)
  blackberries
– 4 tablespoons white wine
– 4½ cups (1½ lb/650 g)
  strawberries
– 2 tablespoons freshly
  squeezed lemon juice,
  strained
– 1½ cups (6½ oz/180 g)
  confectioners' (icing) sugar
– generous 2 cups (17 fl oz/
  500 ml) heavy (double)
  cream, plus extra to decorate
  (optional)

TO DECORATE

– raspberries
– wild strawberries
– blackberries
– 1 sprig lemon balm
  (optional)
– whipped cream (optional)

Put the gelatin into a small bowl of cold water and let stand for 5 minutes to soften. Rinse the wild strawberries and blackberries with the white wine and pat dry with paper towels (kitchen paper). Put the strawberries and wild strawberries into a blender and process to a puree, then transfer to a large bowl.

Put the blackberries into a blender and process to a puree, then pass through a fine nylon strainer (sieve) into the same bowl. Stir in the lemon juice and confectioners' (icing) sugar. Squeeze out the gelatin and put it into a heatproof bowl set over a saucepan of barely simmering water until it has dissolved completely for 2–3 minutes. Gently stir it into the fruit puree.

Whip the cream in another bowl or electric mixer to stiff peaks, then fold it into the fruit mixture. Pour into individual serving glasses and chill in the refrigerator for 6–8 hours, or preferably overnight, until set.

To serve, decorate with fruit, lemon balm leaves, and whipped cream, if desired.

Tip: A bavarois, or Bavarian cream, is a simple dessert usually made with seasonal fruit added to a base of cream. It has the consistency of a custard with the freshness of a summer dessert.

GELO DI MELONE
CHILLED WATERMELON

AVERAGE

– Preparation time: *30 minutes
+ 30 minutes cooling and
4–6 hours chilling*
– Cooking time: *5 minutes*
– Calories per serving: *270*
– *Serves 6*

INGREDIENTS

– ¾ cup (4 oz/115 g)
arrowroot
– ½ cup (3½ oz/100 g)
superfine (caster) sugar
– 4 cups (32 fl oz/950 ml)
watermelon juice
– ½ cups (3½ oz/100 g)
candied pumpkin (zuccata),
diced
– 2 oz/50 g semisweet (plain)
chocolate, coarsely chopped
– jasmine flowers, to decorate
(optional)

Combine the arrowroot and sugar in a saucepan, then gradually stir in the watermelon juice. Set over low heat and bring to a boil, stirring constantly. Cook for 2–3 minutes, until the mixture has thickened, then stir in the candied pumpkin, and remove from the heat. Divide the mixture among 6 small bowls and let cool.

Put 5–6 pieces of chocolate into the mixture in each bowl, then chill in the refrigerator for 4–6 hours.

To serve, briefly dip the bottoms of the bowls in warm water and turn them out onto a serving dish decorated with fresh jasmine flowers, if desired. Alternatively, serve in the bowls.

Note: This is a traditional dish for the Feast of the Assumption on August 15th, both in Palermo and western Sicily. A good "gelo" should be a transparent, fine pink-tinged ruby color and must melt in the mouth.

MELONE SORPRESA
MELON SURPRISE

EASY

- Preparation time: *30 minutes + 2 hours chilling*
- Calories per serving: *250*
- *Serves 6*

INGREDIENTS

- 1 large cantaloupe melon, halved and seeded
- 2 cups (9 oz/250 g) raspberries
- 2⅓ cups (12 oz/350 g) seedless green grapes
- 3 peaches, peeled, pitted, and diced
- ¼ cup (2 oz/50 g) superfine (caster) sugar
- 5 tablespoons sweet liqueur, such as maraschino

Scoop out balls of the melon flesh using a melon baller and place in a bowl. Set aside the half-melon shells. Add the raspberries, grapes, and peaches to the melon balls and sprinkle with the sugar and liqueur. Divide the fruit salad between the melon shells and chill in the refrigerator for at least 2 hours before serving.

ASPIC ALLA PESCA
PEACH ASPIC

AVERAGE

– Preparation time: *30 minutes*
  + 2 hours chilling
– Cooking time: *20 minutes*
– Calories per serving: *490*
– *Serves 4*

INGREDIENTS

– 3 sheets gelatin
– 3 ripe yellow peaches, pitted
  and cut into eighths
– ½ cup (4 fl oz/120 ml)
  amaretto or other liqueur
– 1 cup (7 oz/200 g) superfine
  (caster) sugar
– scant 1 cup (5 oz/150 g)
  chopped candied (glace)
  fruit, plus extra for
  decorating (optional)

Put the gelatin sheets into a small bowl of cold water and let soak for 5 minutes.

Meanwhile, put the peaches into a bowl, sprinkle with the liqueur, and chill in the refrigerator.

Pour generous 2 cups (17 fl oz/500 ml) water into a small saucepan, add the sugar, and bring to a boil over medium heat, stirring, until the sugar has dissolved. Squeeze out the gelatin and add it to the pan, then add the water from the bowl. Bring to a boil, stirring to dissolve the gelatin, then remove the pan from the heat. Stir in the candied fruit, if using, and let stand for 5 minutes. Pour one-third of the mixture into a container and chill for 30 minutes, until it begins to set.

Remove the bowl from the refrigerator, arrange half the peach slices on the gelatin, cover with half the remaining liquid, and return to the refrigerator for 30 minutes. Repeat with the remaining peaches and liquid, return to the refrigerator, and chill for 1 hour, or until set.

To serve, turn out onto a serving dish and decorate with the remaining candied fruit, if using.

VINO GELATO ALLA FRAGOLA
CHILLED WINE WITH STRAWBERRIES

EASY

– Preparation time: *15 minutes*
  + 3 hours chilling
– Calories per serving: *110*
– *Serves 6*

INGREDIENTS

– juice of 2 lemons, strained
– 3–4 sprigs mint
– 6 strawberries, hulled and
  quartered
– superfine (caster) sugar,
  for sprinkling
– 1 bottle dry white wine,
  chilled

Mix the lemon juice with generous 2 cups (17 fl oz/ 500 ml) water in a large bowl. Fill each section of an ice-cube tray halfway with the mixture and freeze for 1 hour. Put a mint leaf on the surface of each ice cube and fill the tray with the remaining lemon mixture. Return to the freezer and freeze for 2 hours.

Put the strawberries into a small bowl and sprinkle with the sugar. To serve, put 2 lemon-flavored ice cubes in each glass, pour in the wine, and decorate with the strawberry pieces.

CANNOLI
CANNOLI

ADVANCED

- Preparation time: *30 minutes*
  + 12 hours chilling
- Cooking time: *1 hour*
- Calories per serving: *230*
- *Makes 22*

INGREDIENTS

- 1¼ cups (5 oz/150 g) all-
  purpose (plain) flour, plus
  extra for dusting
- 1 tablespoon lard
- 2 teaspoons white wine
  vinegar
- 3–4 tablespoons Malvasia
  wine
- 3 egg whites
- 1 teaspoon superfine (caster)
  sugar
- vegetable oil, for frying
- salt
- vanilla-flavored confectioners'
  (icing) sugar, to decorate
- 4–5 shelled pistachio nuts,
  slivered, to decorate

FOR THE FILLING

- 4½ cups (2¼ lb/1 kg) ricotta
  romana
- 3⅓ cups (14 oz/400 g)
  confectioners' (icing) sugar
- ¼ cup (2 oz/50 g) candied
  pumpkin (zuccata), diced
- 3 oz/80 g semisweet (plain)
  chocolate, chopped
- 2–3 tablespoons white rum

First, make the filling. Press the ricotta through a strainer (sieve) into a bowl, then add the confectioners' (icing) sugar, and beat with a wooden spoon. Add the candied pumpkin, chocolate, and rum and mix well. Cover with plastic wrap and chill in the refrigerator for 12 hours.

To make the dough, sift the flour with a pinch of salt into a bowl. Add the lard, vinegar, wine, 2 egg whites, and sugar and mix well to form a firm dough. Shape the dough into a ball, wrap in plastic wrap (clingfilm), and let stand for 30 minutes.

Cut the dough into 2–3 pieces and roll each out on a lightly floured surface. Cut out 20–22 squares or stamp out circles with a fluted cookie cutter. Put a cannoli tube diagonally across each square and wrap the dough around it. Beat the remaining egg white and brush a small amount over the dough to seal.

Fill a skillet or frying pan three-quarters with vegetable oil and heat over medium heat. Add the cannoli, seam side down, a few rolls at a time, and cook, turning once, for a few minutes, until golden brown. Remove with a slotted spoon and drain on paper towels (kitchen paper), then let stand until cool enough to handle. Remove the metal tubes and fill the cannoli with the ricotta filling just before serving.

Dust with confectioners' (icing) sugar and decorate at the ends with the pistachio slivers.

Note: Cannolis are Sicilian pastries filled with ricotta cream. You will need about 20 metal cannoli tubes for shaping the dough. These are available from good kitchenware stores.

BAVARESE AL VINO
WINE BAVAROIS

ADVANCED

- Preparation time: *30 minutes*
  + 30 minutes cooling and
  15 minutes chilling
- Cooking time: *40 minutes*
- Calories per serving: *760*
- *Serves 6*

INGREDIENTS

- 2 sheets gelatin
- 5 tablespoons sweet white
  wine
- juice of ½ lemon, strained
- 4 egg yolks
- ¾ cup (5 oz/150 g) superfine
  (caster) sugar
- generous 2 cups (17 fl oz/
  500 ml) heavy (double)
  cream
- 1 store-bought Genoese or
  sponge cake

FOR THE SYRUP

- 5 tablespoons sweet white
  wine
- 1⅔ cups (9 oz/250 g) red
  grapes
- ½ cup (3½ oz/100 g)
  superfine (caster) sugar

Fill a small bowl with water, add the gelatin, and let soak for 5 minutes.

Gently heat the wine and lemon juice in a saucepan.

Beat the egg yolks with the sugar in another saucepan until pale and fluffy. Whisk in the hot wine mixture and heat gently over low heat, stirring constantly, until the mixture is thick enough to coat the back of the spoon. Remove from the heat and let cool slightly.

Drain the gelatin sheets and squeeze out, then stir into the custard and let cool completely.

Whip the cream in a bowl or electric mixer to stiff peaks, then gently fold it into the cold custard. Chill the bavarois in the refrigerator.

To make the syrup, heat the wine, ⅔ cup (3¼ oz/90 g) of the grapes, and the sugar in a pan over low heat, stirring until the sugar has dissolved. Drain and set the grapes aside and reserve the syrup. Place the remaining grapes in a food processor and process to a puree. Strain the puree into the hot syrup, mix well, and let cool slightly.

Divide the cake into two circular halves. Place a cake circle on a serving dish, sprinkle with some of the syrup, spread a layer of bavarois on top, then a layer of the reserved grapes, then another layer of bavarois. Top with the second cake circle and sprinkle with syrup. Spread the remaining bavarois over the whole cake. Keep chilled until ready to serve, then decorate with the remaining grapes.

BUDINO DI FRUTTA IN GELATINA
FRUIT GELATIN

AVERAGE

– Preparation time: *45 minutes,*
  + 10 minutes cooling and
  8 hours chilling
– Cooking time: *15 minutes*
– Calories per serving: *187–140*
– *Serves 6–8*

INGREDIENTS

– 6 sheets gelatin
– juice of 8 oranges, strained
– juice of 2 lemons, strained
– scant ½ cup (3 oz/80 g)
  superfine (caster) sugar
– 3½ cups (1 lb 2 oz/500 g)
  strawberries, hulled
– 1 small melon, halved and
  seeded

Put the gelatin sheets into a small bowl of cold water and let stand for 5 minutes.

Pour the orange and lemon juices into a saucepan, add the sugar, and cook over low heat, stirring constantly, until the sugar has dissolved. Add the prepared gelatin, bring just to a boil, then remove from the heat and strain.

Place the strawberries in a food processor, process to a puree, then strain into a bowl. Stir the puree into the fruit juice mixture, let cool slightly, then pour into a 6¼-cup (50-fl oz/1.5-liter) tube mold or gelatin ring mold. Chill in the refrigerator for several hours, or overnight until set.

Using a melon baller, scoop out balls of the melon flesh. Turn the mold out onto a serving dish, fill the center with the melon balls, and serve.

PANNA COTTA
PANNA COTTA

PANNA COTTA

AVERAGE

– Preparation time: *35 minutes*
 + 4 hours chilling
– Cooking time: *20 minutes*
– Calories per serving: *350*
– *Serves 6*

INGREDIENTS

– 3 sheets gelatin
– scant ½ cup (3½ fl oz/
 100 ml) milk
– 2 cups (16 fl oz/475 ml)
 heavy (double) cream
– ½ cup (3½ oz/100 g)
 superfine (caster) sugar
– 1 vanilla bean (pod), split in
 half lengthwise
– vegetable oil, for brushing

Put the gelatin sheets in a small bowl with cold water for 3–5 minutes. Meanwhile, heat the milk in a saucepan over low heat. Drain and squeeze out the gelatin sheets and add to the milk.

Pour the cream into another saucepan, add the sugar and vanilla bean (pod), and bring to a boil over low heat, stirring constantly. Immediately remove the pan from the heat, remove the vanilla bean, and stir in the milk mixture.

Brush 6 small ramekins with vegetable oil, shaking out any excess, and fill with the mixture. Chill in the refrigerator for at least 4 hours, until set. Turn out onto plates and serve.

TIRAMISU

TIRAMISU

TIRAMISU

AVERAGE

– Preparation time: *50 minutes + 3 hours chilling*
– Calories per serving: *1,010*
– *Serves 6*

INGREDIENTS

– 2 egg whites
– 4 egg yolks
– 1¼ cups (5 oz/150 g) confectioners' (icing) sugar
– 1¾ cups (14 oz/400 g) mascarpone cheese
– 15 (7 oz/200 g) ladyfingers (sponge fingers)
– ¾ cup (6 fl oz/175 ml) freshly brewed extra strong coffee, cooled
– 7 oz/200 g semisweet (plain) chocolate, grated
– unsweetened cocoa powder, for dusting (optional)

Whisk the egg whites in a grease-free bowl or electric mixer to stiff peaks.

Beat the egg yolks and sugar together in another bowl until pale and fluffy. Gently fold in the mascarpone cheese, then the egg whites.

Make a layer of ladyfingers (sponge fingers) on the bottom of a 6¼-cup (50-fl oz/1.5-liter) serving dish and brush them evenly with the coffee. Cover with a layer of the mascarpone cream and sprinkle with a little grated chocolate. Continue making layers until all the ingredients are used, ending with a layer of mascarpone cream and grated chocolate. Dust with unsweetened cocoa powder, if using, and chill in the refrigerator for about 3 hours.

SPUMANTE ALLA FRUTTA
FRUIT IN SPARKLING WINE

EASY

– Preparation time: *10 minutes*
 + 2 hours chilling
– Calories per serving: *320*
– *Serves 16*

INGREDIENTS

– 18 sugar cubes
– Angostura bitters, for
  sprinkling
– 1 kg/2¼ lb mixed fresh
  berries
– generous 2 cups (17 fl oz/
  500 ml) brandy
– 1¼ cups (10 fl oz/300 ml)
  Grand Marnier
– 4 bottles Prosecco or other
  sparkling wine, chilled

Put the sugar cubes into the bottom of a large bowl and sprinkle with a few drops of Angostura bitters. Arrange the fruit on top, drizzle with the brandy and Grand Marnier, cover, and chill in the refrigerator for at least 2 hours.

Just before serving, pour the sparkling wine over the fruit salad and stir gently.

ZUPPA INGLESE
ITALIAN TRIFLE

AVERAGE

- Preparation time: *1 hour
  30 minutes + 1 hour chilling*
- Cooking time: *10 minutes*
- Calories per serving: *370*
- *Serves 6*

FOR THE TRIFLE

- 1 tablespoon red food
  coloring
- 2 tablespoons rum
- 9 oz (250 g) sponge cake,
  sliced

FOR THE
CUSTARD CREAM

- 4 egg yolks
- ½ cup (3½ oz/100 g)
  superfine (caster) sugar
- ¼ cup (1 oz/30 g)
  all-purpose (plain) flour
- 2¼ cups (18 fl oz/550 ml)
  milk
- a few drops of vanilla extract
  or 1 teaspoon lemon zest

TO DECORATE

- Scant ½ cup (3½ fl oz/
  100 ml) heavy (double)
  cream
- mixed candied (crystallized)
  fruit
- grated chocolate or fresh
  berries

To make the custard cream, beat the egg yolks with the sugar in a pan until pale and fluffy. Gradually stir in the flour until evenly mixed. Bring the milk just to boiling point in another pan and add the vanilla or lemon zest, then remove from the heat. Gradually add the hot milk to the egg yolk mixture, then cook over low heat, stirring continuously, for 3–4 minutes, until thickened. Pour the custard into a bowl and let cool, stirring occasionally to prevent a skin from forming. Set aside and reserve 1 cup (8 fl oz/250 ml) of the custard in a separate bowl.

Mix the food coloring with 1 tablespoon water in a shallow dish. Mix the rum with 1 tablespoon water in another shallow dish.

Arrange a layer of sponge cake slices on the bottom of a 6¼-cup (50-fl oz/1.5-liter) glass dish. Sprinkle with the diluted food coloring and pour on a layer of custard. Make another layer of sponge cake, sprinkle with the rum, and pour on another layer of custard. Continue making alternating layers, ending with a layer of sponge cake. Chill in the refrigerator for 1 hour. Remove the bowl from the refrigerator and let stand for about 10 minutes.

Meanwhile, whip the cream in a bowl or electric mixer to stiff peaks. Spread the reserved custard on top of the last layer of sponge cake. Fill a pastry (piping) bag fitted with a star tip (nozzle) with the whipped cream and use to decorate the trifle, then add candied (crystallized) fruit and grated chocolate or fresh berries.

CHARLOTTE AGLI AMARETTI
AMARETTI CHARLOTTE

AVERAGE

– Preparation: *45 minutes +
30 minutes standing and 4–5
hours chilling*
– Calories per serving: *550*
– *Serves 8*

INGREDIENTS

– 9 oz/250 g semisweet (plain)
  chocolate, broken into
  pieces
– 1 egg yolk
– ½ cup (4 fl oz/120 ml) milk
– 1 stick (4 oz/120 g) butter,
  softened
– scant ¼ cup (1½ oz/45 g)
  superfine (caster) sugar
– vegetable oil, for brushing
– 14 oz/400 g small amaretti
  cookies (biscuits)
– 5 tablespoons rum

Melt the chocolate in a heatproof bowl set over a saucepan of barely simmering water, making sure the bottom of the bowl doesn't touch the water.

Put the egg yolk into a bowl. Heat the milk in a saucepan over low heat for 5 minutes until just warm, then quickly stir into the egg yolk. Return the mixture to the pan and cook, stirring, over medium heat until it has a creamlike consistency. Do not let boil. Strain into the melted chocolate and stir until smooth, then let the chocolate mixture stand until it is no longer warm but is still soft.

In another bowl, beat the butter with the sugar until pale and fluffy. Gradually beat in the chocolate mixture. Brush a 2-quart (68-fl oz/2-liter) mold with a little vegetable oil and line with plastic wrap (clingfilm). Place a layer of amaretti cookies (biscuits) on the bottom and part of the way up the sides of the mold and sprinkle with some of the rum. Spoon one-third of the chocolate mixture over the amaretti. Place another layer of amaretti over the chocolate and up the sides. Sprinkle with rum. Crumble some of the amaretti to fill any gaps. Continue layering and sprinkling until you have used all the mixture, amaretti, and rum, finishing with a layer of amaretti. Cover with plastic wrap and chill for 4–5 hours.

Turn out, remove and discard the plastic wrap, and let stand at room temperature for 30 minutes before serving.

CASSATA
SICILIAN CASSATA

- Preparation time: *1 hour +
  24 hours chilling*
- Cooking time: *15 minutes*
- Calories per serving: *672–560*
- *Serves 10–12*

INGREDIENTS

- ⅔ cup (4 oz/ 120 g) chopped
  candied (glacé) fruit, plus
  extra to decorate
- 4 tablespoons white rum
- 4 cups (2¼ lb/1 kg) ricotta
  cheese
- 4¾ cups (24½ oz/700 g)
  confectioners' (icing) sugar
- 4 oz/120 g bittersweet (dark)
  chocolate, chopped
- 10½-inch/26-cm sponge
  cake
- 1–2 tablespoons milk, plus
  more if needed

FOR THE
PISTACHIO PASTE

- ½ cup (2 oz/50 g) finely
  chopped pistachio nuts
- 1½ cups (5 oz/150 g) finely
  chopped almonds
- ½ cup (2 oz/50 g) icing
  confectioners' (icing) sugar
- 2 tablespoons white rum

FOR THE RUM SYRUP

- 1 cup (7 oz/200 g) superfine
  (caster) sugar
- 2 tablespoons white rum

First make the filling. Put the candied (glacé) fruit
into a bowl, add the rum and let soak for 20 minutes.
Meanwhile, beat the ricotta with 1¾ cups (7 oz/200 g)
sugar in a bowl until smooth and even. Drain the glacé
fruit and stir into the ricotta mixture with the chocolate.
Cover the bowl with plastic wrap (clingfilm) and chill in
the refrigerator for 12 hours.

Make the pistachio paste. Put the pistachio nuts,
almonds, sugar, and rum into a blender and process
to a paste.

Make the rum syrup. Pour scant 1 cup (7 fl oz/200 ml)
water into a shallow saucepan, add the sugar and heat
gently, stirring constantly, until the sugar has completely
dissolved. Bring to a boil and boil, without stirring, for a
few minutes, then remove from the heat. Let cool slightly,
then stir in the rum.

Rinse out a 10½-inch/26-cm cake pan with water and
line with plastic wrap. Line the cake sides with the
pistachio paste and press lightly along the sides.

Cut the sponge cake into slices and put half the slices side
by side on the bottom of the prepared cake pan. Drizzle
with half the rum syrup. Cover with the ricotta filling and
top with the remaining sponge cake slices. Drizzle with
the remaining syrup. Cover the pan with plastic wrap and
chill in the refrigerator for 12 hours.

Sift the remaining 3 cups (17½ oz/500 g) confectioners'
sugar into a large bowl, add the milk, and stir until it
forms a smooth and thick white paste. Add more milk
if needed. To serve, invert the cake onto a serving plate,
pour the icing over the cake, and refrigerate for 1 hour.
Decorate with candied fruit.

CHARLOTTE AI FRUTTI DI BOSCO
FRUITS OF THE FOREST CHARLOTTE

AVERAGE

– Preparation time: *45 minutes
+ 30 minutes cooling and
24 hours chilling*
– Cooking time: *35 minutes*
– Calories per serving: *550*
– *Serves 6*

INGREDIENTS

– 4 gelatin sheets
– generous 2 cups (17 fl oz/
500 ml) milk
– a few drops of vanilla extract
– 6 egg yolks
– ¾ cup (5 oz/150 g) superfine
(caster) sugar
– 24 slices sponge cake
– scant ½ cup (3½ fl oz/
100 ml) heavy (double)
cream
– 1⅔ cups (7 oz/200 g)
raspberries
– 1¼ cups (7 oz/200 g) mixed
red currants and black
currants, stripped
– ⅔ cup (3½ oz/100 g)
blueberries
– ⅔ cup (3½ oz/100 g)
strawberries, hulled and
chopped

Soak the gelatin sheets in a small bowl of cold water.

Pour the milk into a saucepan, add the vanilla, and bring to simmering point, then remove from the heat.

Beat the egg yolks with the sugar in another saucepan until pale and fluffy, then gradually stir in the hot milk, whisking continuously. Drain the gelatin, squeeze out, and add to the custard, then cook over low heat, stirring constantly for 5–10 minutes, until the mixture is thick enough to coat the back of the spoon. Remove from the heat and let cool.

Preheat the broiler (grill) and lightly toast the slices of sponge cake, then line the bottom and sides of a 2-quart (68-fl oz/2-liter) mold with them, reserving enough to cover the top.

Whip the cream in a bowl or electric mixer to stiff peaks, then stir into the cooled custard with the fruit. Pour the mixture into the mold and cover with the remaining slices of sponge cake. Cover the mold with aluminum foil and chill in the refrigerator for 24 hours.

INDEX

A

ALMONDS
- almond baskets with strawberry ice cream 123
- Sicilian cassata 170

AMARETTI COOKIES
- amaretti charlotte 169
- amaretto ice cream 58
- zuccotto 124

AMARETTO
- amaretto ice cream 58
- peach aspic 150

AMARETTO LIQUEUR
- zuccotto 124

APRICOTS
- ricotta and apricot cream 141
arance ripiene di gelato 105

ASPIC
- melon and watermelon aspic 138
- peach aspic 150
aspic di anguria e melone 138
aspic alla pesca 150
avocado, yogurt, and honey cream 134

B

BANANAS
- banana ice cream 22
- tricolor ice pops 90
basil sorbet 85
bavarese ai frutti di bosco 145
bavarese al vino 157

BAVAROIS
- fruits of the forest bavarois 145
- wine bavarois 157

BERRIES
- fruit in sparkling wine 165
- fruits of the forest ice cream 25

BLUEBERRIES
- blueberry frozen yogurt 45

BRANDY
- amaretto ice cream 58
- fruit in sparkling wine 165
- ladyfinger dessert with apricot-flavored brandy 112
budino di frutta in gelatina 158

C

CAKE
- fruits of the forest charlotte 173
- ice cream cake with fruit 89
- Italian trifle 166
- Sicilian cassata 170
- wine bavarois 157
Campari ice pops 93
cannoli 154
cannoli 154
caramel ice cream 49

CASSATA
- Sicilian cassata 170
cestini di arance con crema 142
cestini di mandorle con gelato alla fragola 123

chamomile semifreddo 120

CHAMPAGNE
- peach sorbet 70
- rose petal and cream ice cream 54
charlotte agli amaretti 169
charlotte ai frutti di bosco 173

CHARLOTTES
- amaretti charlotte 169
- fruits of the forest charlotte 173
cherry sorbet 77
chilled desserts 9, 126–73

CHOCOLATE
- amaretti charlotte 169
- chilled watermelon 146
- cookies and cream ice cream 41
- custard and chocolate semifreddo 115
- egg custard and chocolate ice cream 19
- ladyfinger dessert with apricot-flavored brandy 112
- mascarpone semifreddo 111
- mint and chocolate ice cream 21
- panforte and spice bread semifreddo 116
- Sicilian cassata 170
- tiramisu 162
- zuccotto 124

COFFEE
- coffee granita with cream 101
- coffee ice cream 37
- mascarpone semifreddo 111
- tiramisu 162
cookies and cream ice cream 41
cream 10
- coffee granita with cream 101
- cookies and cream ice cream 41
- figs with cream 137
- orange cups with cream 142
- panna cotta 9
- ricotta and apricot cream 141
- rose petal and cream ice cream 54
- wine bavarois 157
- zabaglione ice cream 57
- zuccotto 124
crema alla ricotta e albicocche 141
crema di yogurt al miele e avocado 134
crema gelata al melone 33

CUSTARD
- custard and chocolate semifreddo 115
- egg custard and chocolate ice cream 19
- Italian trifle 166

D

DRINKS
- chilled wine with strawberries 153

E

eggs 10
- egg custard and chocolate ice

cream 19
equipment 12–13

F

fichi alla crema 137
figs with cream 137
flavoring ingredients 10
forks 12
frozen desserts 86–125

FRUIT
- fruit gelatin 158
- fruit in sparkling wine 165
- fruit salad with ice cream 129
- fruits of the forest bavarois 145
- fruits of the forest charlotte 173
- fruits of the forest ice cream 25
- ice cream cake with fruit 89
- mixed fruit ice cream 106

G

GELATIN
- fruit gelatin 158 159
gelato ai biscotti e yogurt 41
gelato ai fiori di gelsomino 65
gelato ai frutti di bosco 25
gelato al caffè 37
gelato al caramello 49
gelato al croccante di nocciole 46
gelato al Parmigiano 62
gelato al pistacchio con fragoline di bosco 34
gelato al tè 38
gelato al torrone con uvette e vino 53
gelato al vino di Malaga 61
gelato all'amaretto 58
gelato all'ananas 29
gelato alla banana 22
gelato alla crema e cioccolato 19
gelato alla fragole 42
gelato alla mandarino 26
gelato alla menta e cioccolato 21
gelato alla panna e petali di rosa 54
gelato alla pesca 30
gelato alle fragoline e limone 50
gelato allo yogurt con mirtilli 45
gelato allo zabaione 57
gelo di melone 146

GENOESE SPONGE
- wine bavarois 157
ghiaccioli al campari 93
ghiaccioli "spiritosi" 94
ghiaccioli tricolore 90

GOLDEN RAISINS
- nougat ice cream with golden raisins and wine 53

GRAND MARNIER
- fruit in sparkling wine 165
- panforte and spice bread semifreddo 116

GRANITA 9
- coffee granita with cream 101
- peach granita 97
- raspberry and red currant granita 98
granita al caffè con panna 101
granita alla pesca 97
granita al lamponi e ribes 98

GRAPEFRUIT JUICE
- greyhound ice pops 94

GRAPES
- fruit salad with ice cream 129
- melon surprise 149
- wine bavarois 157

GRENADINE SYRUP
- mixed fruit ice cream 106
greyhound ice pops 94

H

HAZELNUTS
- avocado, yogurt, and honey cream 134
- cookies and cream ice cream 41
- praline ice cream 46

HONEY
- avocado, yogurt, and honey cream 134

I

ice cream 9, 16–65
- almond baskets with strawberry ice cream 123
- amaretto ice cream 58
- banana ice cream 22
- blueberry frozen yogurt 45
- caramel ice cream 49
- cantaloupe frozen yogurt 33
- coffee ice cream 37
- cookies and cream ice cream 41
- egg custard and chocolate ice cream 19
- fruit salad with ice cream 129
- fruits of the forest ice cream 25
- ice cream cake with fruit 89
- jasmine ice cream 65
- Malaga wine ice cream 61
- mint and chocolate ice cream 21
- mixed fruit ice cream 106
- nougat ice cream with golden raisins and wine 53
- oranges filled with ice cream 105
- Parmesan ice cream 62
- peach ice cream 30
- pineapple ice cream 29
- pistachio ice cream with wild strawberries 34
- plums with ice cream 133
- praline ice cream 46
- rose petal and cream ice cream 54
- strawberry ice cream 42
- tangerine ice cream 26
- tea ice cream 38
- wild strawberry and lemon ice cream 50
- zabaglione ice cream 57

ice cream makers 12, 14
ice pop molds 12
ice pops 9
– Campari ice pops 93
– greyhound ice pops 94
– tricolor ice pops 90
ingredients 10
Italian trifle 166

J

jasmine ice cream 65

K

KIWI FRUIT
– kiwi sorbet 78
– tricolor ice pops 90

L

LADYFINGERS
– ladyfinger dessert with
  apricot-flavored brandy 112
– tiramisu 162
LEMONS
– lemon sorbet 69
– Prosecco sorbet 82
– wild strawberry and lemon ice
  cream 50

M

macedonia con gelato 129
Malaga wine ice cream 61
MALVASIA WINE
– cannoli 154
MARASCHINO
– melon surprise 149
MARSALA
– chamomile semifreddo 120
– zabaglione semifreddo 119
MASCARPONE CHEESE
– mascarpone semifreddo 111
– tiramisu 162
mattonella di savoiardi all'apricot
  112
MELON
– cantaloupe frozen yogurt 33
– fruit gelatin 158
– melon and watermelon
  aspic 138
– melon balls with mint-
  flavored yogurt 130
– melon surprise 149
melone sorpresa 149
milk 10
MINT
– chilled wine with strawberries
  153
– melon balls with mint-
  flavored yogurt 130
– mint and chocolate ice
  cream 21
molds 12

N

NECTARINES
– fruit salad with ice cream 129
– ice cream cake with fruit 89
nougat ice cream with golden
  raisins and wine 53

O

ORANGES
– Campari ice pops 93
– fruit gelatin 158
– orange cups with cream 142
– orange sorbet 73
– oranges filled with ice cream
  105

P

paciugo® 106
palline di melone con yogurt
  alla menta 130
PAN DI SPAGNA
– zuccotto 124
panforte and spice bread
  semifreddo 116
panna cotta 161
panna cotta 161
pans 12
Parmesan ice cream 62
PEACHES
– melon surprise 149
– peach aspic 150
– peach granita 97
– peach ice cream 30
– peach sorbet 70
pineapple ice cream 29
PISTACHIO NUTS
– oranges filled with ice cream
  105
– pistachio ice cream with wild
  strawberries 34
– Sicilian cassata 170
plastic wrap 12
PLUMS
– plum sorbet 74
– plums with ice cream 133
PORT
– zabaglione ice cream 57
praline ice cream 46
PROSECCO
– basil sorbet 85
– fruit in sparkling wine 165
– melon and watermelon
  aspic 138
– Prosecco sorbet 82
prugne con gelato 133

R

RAISINS
– amaretto ice cream 58
RASPBERRIES
– iced raspberry and strawberry
  souffle 102
– melon surprise 149
– raspberry and red currant
  granita 98
– raspberry semifreddo 108
RED CURRANTS
– raspberry and red currant
  granita 98
RICOTTA CHEESE
– ricotta and apricot cream 141
– Sicilian cassata 170
rose petal and cream ice
  cream 54
RUM
– amaretti charlotte 169

– cookies and cream ice
  cream 41
– Italian trifle 166
– peach ice cream 30
– Sicilian cassata 170

S

semifreddo 9
– chamomile semifreddo 120
– custard and chocolate
  semifreddo 115
– mascarpone semifreddo 111
– panforte and spice bread
  semifreddo 116
– raspberry semifreddo 108
– zabaglione semifreddo 119
semifreddo al lampone 108
semifreddo al mascarpone 111
semifreddo al panforte e pan di
  spezie 116
semifreddo alla camomilla 120
semifreddo alla crema e cioccolato
  115
semifreddo allo zabaione 119
SHERRY
– nougat ice cream with golden
  raisins and wine 53
Sicilian cassata 170
sorbet 9, 66–85
– basil sorbet 85
– cherry sorbet 77
– kiwi sorbet 78
– lemon sorbet , 69
– orange sorbet 73
– peach sorbet 70
– plum sorbet 74
– Prosecco sorbet 82
– tropical sorbet 81
sorbetto al basilico 85
sorbetto al kiwi 78
sorbetto al limone 69
sorbetto al prosecco 82
sorbetto all'arancia 73
sorbetto alla pesca 70
sorbetto di ciliegie 77
sorbetto di prugne 74
sorbetto tropicale 81
SOUFFLE
– iced raspberry and strawberry
  souffle 102
soufflé gelato al lampone e fragola
  102
SPICE BREAD
– panforte and spice bread
  semifreddo 116
spumante alla frutta 165
strainers 13
STRAWBERRIES
– almond baskets with
  strawberry ice cream 123
– chilled wine with strawberries
  153
– iced raspberry and strawberry
  souffle 102
– pistachio ice cream with wild
  strawberries 34
– strawberry ice cream 42
– wild strawberry and lemon ice
  cream 50
sugar 10

T

tangerine ice cream 26
tea ice cream 38
techniques 14
tiramisù 162
tiramisu 162
torta gelato alla frutta 89
tricolor ice pops 90
TRIFLE
– Italian trifle 166
tropical sorbet 81

V

vino gelato alle fragola 153
VODKA
– greyhound ice pops 94

W

WAFERS
– ice cream cake with fruit 89
WATERMELON
– chilled watermelon 146
– fruit salad with ice cream 129
– melon and watermelon
  aspic 138
whisks 12
WINE
– chilled wine with strawberries
  153
– fruit in sparkling wine 165
– fruits of the forest bavarois
  145
– Malaga wine ice cream 61
– nougat ice cream with golden
  raisins and wine 53
– tropical sorbet 81
– wine bavarois 157
– *see also* champagne; Prosecco

Y

YOGURT
– avocado, yogurt, and honey
  cream 134
– blueberry frozen yogurt 45
– cantaloupe frozen yogurt 33
– cookies and cream ice
  cream 41
– melon balls with mint-
  flavored yogurt 130
– strawberry ice cream 42

Z

zabaglione ice cream 57
zabaglione semifreddo 119
zuccotto 124
zuccotto 124
zuppa inglese 166

Recipe Notes

Butter should always
be unsalted.

Eggs are assumed to be
extra-large (UK: large) size,
unless otherwise specified.

Milk is always whole
(full-fat), unless otherwise
specified.

Cooking and preparation
times are only for guidance,
because individual ovens vary.
If using a convection (fan)
oven, follow the manufacturer's instructions concerning
oven temperatures.

Some recipes include
raw or very lightly cooked
eggs. These should be
avoided particularly by
the elderly, infants, pregnant
women, convalescents,
and anyone with an impaired
immune system.

All spoon measurements
are level. 1 teaspoon = 5 ml;
1 tablespoon = 15 ml. Australian standard tablespoons are
20 ml, so Australian readers
are advised to use 3 teaspoons
in place of 1 tablespoon when
measuring small quantities.

Cup, metric, and imperial
measurements are given
throughout, and UK equiva-
lents are given in brackets.
Follow one set of measurements, not a mixture, because
they are not interchangeable.

Phaidon Press Limited
Regent's Wharf
All Saints Street
London N1 9PA

Phaidon Press Inc.
65 Bleecker Street
New York, NY 10012

www.phaidon.com

First published 2016
© 2016 Phaidon Press Limited

ISBN: 978 07148 7121 9

Italian Cooking School Ice Cream originates from *Il cucchiaio
d'argento*, first published in 1950, eighth edition (revised, expanded,
and updated in 1997); *Il cucchiaio d'argento estate*, first published in
2005; *Il cucchiaio d'argento cucina regionale*, first published in 2008;
Scuola di cucina gelati, conserve e dolci di frutta, first published in
2013. © Editoriale Domus S.p.A. and Cucchiaio s.r.l.

A CIP catalogue record for this book is available from
the British Library.

Commissioning Editor: Emilia Terragni
Project Editor: Michelle Meade
Production Controller: Amanda Mackie
Designed by Atlas

Photography © Phaidon Press: Liz and Max Haarala Hamilton 6, 8,
20, 23, 27, 28, 35, 36, 39, 40, 43, 44, 47, 48, 51, 52, 55, 56, 59, 60, 63,
64, 71, 72, 76, 79, 83, 84, 91, 95, 96, 99, 104, 109, 113, 114, 117, 118,
121, 122, 139, 140, 143; Steven Joyce 135, 144; Edward Park 125,
128, 154, 156, 159, 160, 163, 164, 167, 168, 171, 172; Andy Sewell 24,
31, 32, 75, 103, 107, 131, 132, 135, 147, 148, 151, 152

Photography © Editoriale Domus S.p.A. and Cucchiaio d'Argento
S.r.l.: Archivio Cucchiaio d'Argento s.r.l. 11, 13, 15, 18, 68, 80, 88,
92, 100, 110

Printed in Romania

The publisher would like to thank Carmen Figini, Ellie Smith,
Astrid Stavro, Gemma Wilson, Susan Spaull, Theresa Bebbington,
Kate Blinman, Rebecca Wilkinson, Elizabeth Clinton, and Lena
Hall for their contributions to the book.